WHAT OTHERS ARE SAYING

"Grief is tough and this book helps one focus on healing. Gates gives insights and asks questions that helps one know where they are in the process of healing. The insights give hope to a better tomorrow. He coaches us to this better tomorrow because he has experienced life through the pits of grief. Thanks, Coach Allan Gates for giving us these truths."

—Charlie Baker
Executive Coach with Ernst and Young

Allan writes, "Grief is the universal experience that is common to every person." He knows what he is talking about. The practical insights found in this book come from his own journey through the valley of the shadow of death.

—Dr. Phil Neighbors
Senior Pastor Valley Baptist Church
Bakersfield California

You were NOT born to write this book....you were shaped to! I loved everything. It was real.... it was frank...it was challenging and it was RAW, while ultimately bringing, hope, truth, comfort and the journey to a place of understanding and healing! If life has taught me anything, it's that DEATH NEVER ARRIVES ON TIME! And, that the loss creates a death in us, that must be resurrected before we can live on! I believe this book will help whoever reads it and answers the call do just that. I'll do anything to help as many read this as possible....

—Michael Delgiorno
On Air Radio Personality

Great information, but what an excellent set of practical tools to navigate the sometimes complicated and painful path that grief creates.

—Jerry N. Duncan, PhD,
ABPPBoard Certified Psychologist

This book is needed on so many levels for those who deal with grief. My pastor, Dr. Phil Jett, used to say, "You are either in a storm, headed into storm, or coming out of a storm." Dr. Allan Gates' book will be your rain boots as you traipse through the mud and muck of your storm or help others walk through theirs. Having spent the last twenty-four years of my life on staff at a local church and in vocational ministry, it is my opinion that every minister ought to read and recommend this practical, inspirational, and necessary book. This is the how to book with a heart that you have been looking for.

—Denise Lopez,
Founder EveryDay Ministries

If you've ever asked the question "Where's God?", then you're not alone. All of us are touched by tragedy in some way during our life here on this earth, and Allan Gates is no exception. After losing his spouse at a young age, his grief was overwhelming. But he soon found his grief matched by God's grace. He met Patricia, who was recovering from the loss of a spouse herself, and they joined together to help each other cope and recover.

Allan has bravely put to pen the principles he learned during those hardest days of his life. In Where's God? A Personal Discovery Through Grief and Suffering, he explores the depth of loss and the power of God that transformed him.

So, where is God? Well, I can tell you I've seen him. Every time I'm with Allan and Pat, I see God working through their life. I see God in the work they do to help families heal and move forward. I see God in the way their own family has grown through grief into shining examples of God's love for all humanity.

I hope this book will find you if you're in a place you never thought you'd be. Because I know that God wants to change you, just like he has Allan.

—Dr Alex Himaya
Senior Pastor, thechurch.at

WHERE'S GOD?

WHERE'S GOD?

A PERSONAL DISCOVERY
THROUGH GRIEF AND SUFFERING

DR. ALLAN GATES

Published by Tate Publishing & Enterprises, LLC
127 E. Trade Center Terrace | Mustang, Oklahoma 73064 USA
1.888.361.9473 | www.tatepublishing.com

Tate Publishing is committed to excellence in the publishing industry. The company reflects the philosophy established by the founders, based on Psalm 68:11,
"The Lord gave the word and great was the company of those who published it."

Cover design by Arjay Grecia
Interior design by Jomel Pepito

Published in the United States of America

ISBN: 978-1-62854-210-3
1. Religion / General
2. Religion / Christian Life / Death, Grief, Bereavement
14.07.25

ACKNOWLEDGMENTS

Cheryl and Steven were precious people who loved God, served God, and just wanted to see their children grow up. They never got the opportunity. It gives Pat and me added responsibility to make sure Matthew, Alisha, Jason, and Jonathan are given the opportunity the departed parent wanted them to have.

Pat has been the one constant and consistent human being in my life. She has taught me the power of prayer. She is the rock of the family. She sees the good in everyone and goes out of her way to make sure everyone is taken care of at all times. I couldn't have asked for a better partner in life.

Our friends have been a major support in our new family structure, and I would like to mention them and one of the roles they have played in our life. In no particular order:

Sybil and Thurman Allen—thank you for taking care of our children so that Pat and I could go on vacation to get to know one another. Thank you for accepting me in your family.

Ron and Corrie Egge—thank you for being a couple who stepped in to a hurting family and stepped up to help a new family form.

Dennis and Donna Johnson—our "heart friends" that faithfully help us with premarital couples and are so willing to be our "vacation travel partners."

Dwayne and Tonya Thompson—invited us to Montana to speak at our first marriage conference. You have been faithful friends through the years.

Charlie Baker—thanks for being my "pastor," friend, and encourager in a difficult time of my life.

Jerry Duncan—thank you for never giving up on me, even in the darkest period of life.

Larry Wileman—thank you for spending time with me in a spiritual mentor relationship.

Michael Delgerono—a friend for a reason and a specific season. Best road tripper ever.

Phil and Cindy Neighbors—proof that something good can come out of Lake Creek, Oklahoma. Thanks for your support and encouragement.

Denise and Carl Lopez—thank you for the ministry to our children.

Caleb and Jodi Steele—a couple of influence. One of the best role models for marriage that we have ever been associated with. It will be a pleasure to see what God will do with you.

Richard and Joyce Watts—convinced us to "saddle up" (Joyce) and go international to speak on marriage. You encouraged us to have one of the best experiences of life.

Jon and Meggan Warren—supported our endeavor to start in the marriage-speaking arena. You were my first co-speaker at marriage seminars. You guys are an example of how marriage is supposed to work.

Julie and Jim Carney—a couple who loves each other and gives love to us. Possibly one of the top ten couples I have ever met in life.

Scott and Marlynn Pruitt—the only reason I still believe in politics. This is a couple called by God to do what they do for life. Thank you for loving and supporting us.

CONTENTS

FOREWORD

Cheryl, my wife, died in the prime of her life. She developed adult respiratory distress syndrome and died in a matter of thirty days. I could not believe it! We were active in our Christian life, our church, our family, and our community. How could God allow this to happen? Didn't He understand how my life had just been totally destroyed? My simple answers of "Who is God?" all of a sudden didn't work anymore. Those who provided answers were as wrong as they could be. I was drifting off in my personal emotional pain, grieving, and angry at God. The poems in this book were written by me during this time.

One day, in my suffering, God provided a miracle. The miracle had a name, Pat, who was much farther in her grieving process than I. Her husband, Steven, had died of a fast-growing cancer.

We formed a family born in grief. We brought four children (Matthew, Alisha, Jason, Jonathan) together to each experience grief in their own way. They learned, just as you will, to experience the grief journey. We must each answer the question, "Where's God?" in this process.

We can't spend one day on this earth without learning of another event: a school shooting, a hurricane, a tornado, rape, senseless killing of human beings, or unexplainable deaths.

When a tragedy occurs in the news, something that really shakes you to the core, it affects you even if you weren't there or didn't know any of the victims personally. It has the power to change you. Perhaps after a tragic event, you'll look at your relationships differently. Maybe you'll take more time with people and show them patience, or perhaps you'll see friends and family a little differently. Perhaps you will seek to experience God in a different, more meaningful way.

We all experience personal tragedy in one form or another. The experience of the death of my spouse at an early age has changed the course of my life.

You may be sad after a news event, even though you weren't part of the tragedy. Senseless acts will draw you in and make you imagine yourself or your loved ones in a similar situation.

You may also feel the need to do something. That's why I wrote this book. This book is for those who help and those who need help to begin the journey of personal grief recovery. I also felt the need to do something bigger than myself with this book. Therefore, I want you to know the proceeds of this book are going to help others in the world. The proceeds will go to EveryDay Ministry, Inc.

The mission statement of this ministry organization is to:

1. Do whatever, wherever, however and for whoever God leads; and to encourage and empower others to do the same.
2. Always give more than the gospel but never less than the gospel in all that we do.
3. Use every day needs to share the gospel.

Right now the ministry is focusing on the country of Ghana.

EveryDay Ministry, Inc. is helping local pastors plant churches in remote villages in West Africa, most of which have never heard the gospel. The ministry provides water wells, pole barns (which are used as school houses during the week and churches on Sundays) doing medical clinics, and supplying everyday basic needs in order to transform these villages.

The ministry also works with an existing home for girls who have been rescued from sex trafficking. The home is called The Frankadua Girls Home. The girls can stay up to three years. They receive extensive counseling, discipleship training, education, and training in an occupation.

The ministry is exploring micro financing as a way to help these girls buy their own places of business when they graduate from the home.

When you buy this book, you are purchasing a chance for others to walk through the grieving process.

Here, there, or Ghana, people are people who need help with the grieving process.

—Dr. Allan Gates

For more information on EveryDay Ministry, Inc. or to find out how you can help to make a difference visit EveryDayMinistry.net or contact Denise@everydayministry.net.

I look forward to your comments on this book by emailing me at: allangatesauthor@gmail.com

LOSS

Cheryl was a beautiful, thirty-four-year-old, deeply committed Christian. She was the mother of two sons, ages ten and six. She was a registered nurse who worked in a neonatal intensive care unit. She was a strong witness for Jesus Christ. She had an ongoing marriage of fourteen years. She was an active member of a Bible-believing church. She had a quiet ministry. She ministered to people in her neighborhood and at work. Whenever new people moved into her neighborhood, she helped them find healthcare and presented the gospel. She had begun a Bible study with a woman who had recently found a relationship with Christ. This quiet Christian woman hardly ever won awards but was voted "Working Woman" of the month by a local radio station. She shared her faith with the on-air radio personality. She always tried to rearrange her work schedule so she could be at home when her sons were out of school. It has been said that Cheryl was one of those rare people who didn't have enemies.

One September morning, she awoke with a headache. As the day progressed, she ended up being hospitalized with pneumonia. After three days, she was transferred to intensive care. Even after many dosages of antibiotics, nothing seemed to stop the process of her lungs hardening. The physicians from family practice, to internal medicine, to infection medicine specialists could not find a cure. In a matter of twenty-eight days, this lively woman bested modern medicine and went home to be with the Lord. The question of "fairness" could well be argued by her husband, children, parents, brother, sister, and close friends. Did God allow her death? Did "just life being unfair" win out? Did God know she was going to die? What purpose was served by her tragic loss? Why would God permit this to happen to Cheryl? Isn't this illogical and inconsistent with the theology that God takes care of us? The continued conflict for the family came in waves: "You are now alone," "You must struggle through life alone," "Who are you?" "How do you fit in?" "God has abandoned you," "God is not all-powerful!"

Steven was an energetic, handsome, thirty-four-year-old father of two young children—a son, twelve and a daughter, ten. He was a Sunday-school teacher in the youth department and an active deacon in his church. Steven had a daily walk with the Lord that showed in everything he did—at home, at work, and at play. He was a good listener and always made you feel like he had time for you no matter what was going on around him. Steven was actively involved with his children and was in the process of building a new house. He and his wife had been married for almost sixteen years, and he had a promising career as a civil engineer. Everything seemed to be going his way. God appeared to be richly blessing this family.

Gradually, his energy level began dropping. He began to lose weight and attributed it to the heavy schedule of working and building a house. Steven went to the doctor upon developing a slight cough, because he didn't have time to get sick and thought he should catch this cold before it became serious. But it was already serious; Steven found out a few days later that he had non-Hodgkin's lymphoma—cancer. The oncologist said it was just "garden variety lymphoma" and with a few treatments of chemotherapy, there should be no trouble getting it under control. Steven's cancer had been detected so early; he was so healthy, having rarely been sick, and so young that it should not have been a problem to reduce the small cancerous nodes in his glands.

After all, the cancer had not spread to any other parts of his body; so this treatment would surely cure the problem. However, the doctor and Steven's plans were not God's plan. After just a few treatments of chemotherapy, the doctors discovered that Steven's cancer was not going to go away so quickly; it began to spread throughout his bloodstream and throughout his body. Steven was not going to give up hope knowing that God was still in control in even the bleakest times. He was in the hospital several times, the last time for seven weeks. He daily spent time in prayer and Bible study and shared with the many friends and coworkers who came to visit during the long hospital stay. They could not understand how Steven could still smile after all the chemotherapy treatments, blood transfusions, bouts of nausea, medicines, etc., that he was exposed to day in and day out.

They would ask and he would tell them about his relationship with the one who could miraculously heal him, his lord and savior, Jesus Christ. Steven always told them that God could heal him either here on earth or in heaven. It appeared to all that God would work a miracle and heal him on earth so he could continue his ministry and show all those nonbelievers that God does answer prayer.

God's answer to prayer is not always the answer we expect. God did heal Steven by taking him home to be with Him on one April evening, seven months after he was diagnosed. His wife, children, family, and friends were stunned. Why did God decide to answer their prayers that way? Steven was needed so much here on earth. Why did a good Christian man have to die when so many mean men still live? It wasn't fair, and they didn't understand. Who was this God that stated, "Do not fear, for I am with you; Do not be anxious for I am your God. I will strengthen you, I will help you, I will hold you with my victorious right hand" (Isa. 41:10).

Because people have a need to provide an explanation, well-meaning wishers told these two families something like these: "God is trying to teach you something out of this experience," "You should be privileged that God is giving you the opportunity to lean on him," "I know exactly how you feel," "You should be thankful you had them for *X* amount of time," "Mediate on the blessing you still enjoy," "Be thankful you have children," "In time you'll get over it," "You're undergoing a training session to be a better soldier for God," "Someone else is worse off than you," "Let me tell you how (my relative) died."

It's true these comments each contain an element of truth, but this helpful advice does nothing to answer the questions of the person in emotional pain. It may be the right medicine, but it's being dispensed at the wrong time. The grief process for the immediate family members, extended family, and hurting faithful friends begins when physical life ends.

The very thing happened to C.S. Lewis, a brilliant English scholar who was a proclaimed atheist, became convinced of the truth of Christianity. Lewis married and watched his wife die of cancer only three years after their wedding. In his book *A Grief Observed,* which Lewis wrote after that experience, he began openly explaining his disappointment in friends and family members. Lewis told others in the book to be cautious of those who would provide easy answers to difficult questions.

Don't tell me!!!
Don't tell me you know how I feel,
You haven't been in my grief.
Don't tell me I have others to love,
That won't bring back the one that I lost.
Don't tell me to get out and be active,
Maybe I just want to stay
here and think or pray
Don't tell me time will heal
For me it will never be real.

Don't tell me it could be worse,
How would you know?
Don't tell me to trust in God,
I can't even see Him at this time.
Don't tell me to eat and take care of myself,
Food doesn't sustain my emotions.
Don't tell me that I need rest,
My sleep is all but disturbed.
Don't tell me,
You don't know
Do tell me that you love me.

GRIEF DEFINED

Grief is such a disorderly process. It comes because of trauma, bad experiences, death, and any number of negative experiences. It comes on you in waves, in circles, in spirals. It rarely happens from point *A* to point *B*. You move forward one day and take two steps back the next day. You seem to be leaving the intense-pain stage only to return to the intense-pain stage. You are not normal. Your life is totally disruptive. You can't think straight. You don't act right. You say and do things that are out of character. You are easily distracted, and you appear disoriented. Time stands still. You don't seem to have a past or future, only the pain of the present.

Grief is the deep and poignant distress caused by a natural or unnatural tragic event. Grief is the normal and natural response to loss. Grief is the real emotional pain you feel by the loss of a loved one. Grief is the universal experience that is common to every person, race, or creed. Grief is that conflicting mass of human emotions that we experience following any major change in a familiar pattern of behavior. Grief is a common experience to us all. The only persons who escape grief are those who die before they form loving relationships. Everyone you meet is grieving some kind of loss. We grieve for the loss of all relationships that could be held as significant and therefore emotional: moving to another community, moving to another stage of the life cycle, children leaving home, changing jobs, financial ups and downs, losing your physical or mental health. Often, these common life experiences are not recognized as loss; and so the person who suffers is not aware of the emotional impact, but is aware of the strange feelings associated with the event. Grief is included in the Scripture known as the Beatitudes. "Blessed are those that mourn, for they shall be comforted" (Matt. 5:4).

The only persons who are incapable of grief are those unable to experience love and affection. The capacity to love entails the experience of grief at some point in life. The experience of grief indicates the ability to care and relate to other persons. It also entails the ability to enjoy God's gifts to us, the people in life whom we cherish, and the extent to which we miss them when lost.

We have all experienced the process of loss. Each new stage in the life cycle brings opportunity for loss. Our earliest childhood experiences teach us about loss. When we are born we cry for the safe surroundings that were once our whole existence. We lose our childhood innocence, our adolescence, our responsibilities, and our adult unfulfilled dreams and wishes. We begin to accept our mind and body limitations all the while "acting out" to regain our youth. Grief affects us, others around us, and our core belief in God.

Along Grief's Journey
I hear all the noise in my head
and the noise gives my sense of self nothing
but pain.
I know one day the noise will be gone,
and I must learn to live again.
People keep shopping at the store,
They don't even realize you're gone.
My life has changed,
All of a sudden I can't go on.
One day I will build my new life.
How long does this pain last? I cry out to God
He doesn't hear, and I die all over again.

John Claypool, a pastor, wrote a classic on grief *Tracks of a Fellow Struggler* as he experienced firsthand his eight-year-old daughter go through the process of dying from leukemia. Claypool tells of sitting beside his daughter's bed hour after hour, and shouting, "Just what on earth do You think that You are doing in all of this anyway? I quit. I give up. I can't stand the pain anymore. Stop the world I want to get off." Claypool goes on to say,

> I do not believe God wants me to hold back my questions that burn in my heart and soul—questions like: "Why is there leukemia?" "Why are children of promise cut down at age eight?" "Why did she have to suffer for two years and then die?" I am really honoring God

> when I come clean and say, "You owe me an explanation." For, you see, I believe God will be able to give such an accounting when all the facts are in, and until then, it is valid to ask. (Claypool, 1995, p.53)

Not only is it valid to ask questions of God, but it is necessary that we ask questions of ourselves in the process.

GRIEF SELF-ASSESSMENT

1. How do I expect to be feeling at this stage of my grieving?
   a. Better than I am______
   b. About right________
   c. Probably could be doing worse________

2. My loss was?
   a. Totally unexpected________
   b. Expected, but I was unprepared._________
   c. Expected, but I had time to prepare._______

3. This loss was how long ago?
   a. Years________
   b. Months_________
   c. Recent (days or weeks) _____

4. What I believe about this loss?
    a. It was unfair, and I totally lost because of it.______
    b. My life will never be the same.________
    c. My life can be different, but I can't see it yet.________

5. How have you experienced this event?
    a. I don't understand why it happened.______
    b. I understand but don't accept what happened.________
    c. What I feel makes sense in light of what happened.________

6. My feelings since the event?
    a. I am out of control.______
    b. I have times when I am in control.______
    c I am never out of control.______

7. My physical health since the event?
    a. I am not eating or sleeping correctly.______
    b. I am eating/sleeping with the aid of medications._____
    c. I am doing the best I can in this area.________

8. My thinking processes since the event?
   a. I can't find a reason to go on.______
   b. Most days I can think correctly. __________
   c. Some days I can think correctly.______

9. My view of the future?
   a. I don't see a future for me._______
   b. I am hopeful of a future for me.______
   c. Mostly I can see a future for my recovery.________

10. My present view of life?
    a. I drink alcohol and take meds to deal with the pain.______
    b. The pain comes and goes, and I ride the wave._____
    c. I experience a constant dull ache.______

11. My spiritual life since the event?
    a. I blame God._____
    b. I don't know if I can get strength from God.______
    c. I pray and hope for strength.____

12. How do I see myself?
    a. I am hopeless and worthless._______

b. I am a broken person but not hopeless.______
c. I am hopeful._____

13. My dreams when I do sleep?
 a. Nightmares_______
 b. I can't remember dreams. _______
 c. Comforting_______

14. My support system?
 a. I do not have a support system.___
 b. I do have people, but I am not using them to help.______
 c. I am having people help me._______

SCORING

If you scored mostly *c*, you are clearly grieving normally and probably do not need professional help, although you may wish to talk to someone.

If you scored mostly *b*, you have developed some complicated grieving stages that need to be shared with a professional helper. Some professional helpers would include physicians, pastoral staff experienced in dealing with grief issues, and professional therapists.

If you scored mostly *a*, professional help is highly recommended and urgent for you in this stage of the grief process.

> You must answer the questions in an honest manner and commit to share the assessment with at least two other people.
>
> Signature____________________________
>
> Date______________
>
> And these are the two people with whom I will share my answers to this assessment:__________,
> ____
> ____.

I want you to know, there are no right or wrong answers, only the answers that you are able to give about where you are in the process of grief. You must determine what is right and wrong for you. No one can give you the magic formula of how, why, where to grieve. You must be the person to grieve, to talk to others, to reach out to others to help them understand the pain you alone feel. You are the only one who weeps and no one can weep for you. Jesus wept. He let the pain of emotions overwhelm Him when He appeared at the tomb of His close friend. If you try to hold back the pain and grief inside, it can cause terrible medical and physical problems. The best thing you can do for yourself is to pour it out to God. He can handle our anger, our complaining, and our yelling about how unfair this loss is for us. Our tears are helpful and necessary. They allow our soul to cry out when we don't have words to say what we are feeling. Max Lucado in his book *No Wonder They Call Him the Savior* talks about the work of tears in our life.

> Tears. Those tiny drops of humanity. Those round, wet balls of fluid that tumble from our eyes, creep down our cheeks, and splash on the floor of our hearts. They were there that day. They were always present in such times. They should be; that's their job. They are miniature messengers; on call twenty-four hours a day to substitute for crippled words. They drip, drop and pour from the corner of our souls, carrying with them the deepest emotions we possess. They tumble down our faces with announcements that range from the most blissful joy to darkest despair. (Lucado, 1986, pp.105–106)

You will weep again, sometime in the future; it might not be tomorrow, or next week, or next month, but you will weep again. But this weeping will be the tears of joy, peace, happiness. This only happens as you begin to experience the recovering process.

How long before I weep with joy? No one knows. You have never experienced this before. You've not been down this specific road before at this specific time in your life. Not much has prepared you for this encounter with loss. Most victims of loss describe a very loose time frame that looks something like this:

> One to three months: shock, denial, sadness, depression, anger.
>
> Three to six months: bargaining with God to make the pain go away, starting to make a different life.

Six to twelve months: more "good" than "bad" emotional days, making some important decisions.

One year: a wall, the anniversary, constant reminder of what you have lost.

Eighteen months: periods of sadness, sometimes overwhelming emotions.

Every important date: anniversary, birthday, special occasions.

It is important that you not make yourself be on a time schedule. Everyone grieves differently. At some point, you will begin to notice progress in yourself. When it happens, and you can move forward, then move forward. This doesn't depend on some artificial time factor but does depend on your investing time and energy into your new and different life. And it occurs when you are ready. Some people find it helpful to use a mood chart to track progress. Please use as an opportunity to track your progress week by week.

Mood Chart Documentation

Week of: _______________

Severe: I am totally unable to function, stay in bed all day, crying all the time.

Moderate: It takes a lot of effort to carry out even simple tasks.

Mild: I need extra time to complete tasks, but I am functioning in my usual activities.

Stable: I have some bad moments but not all the day. I can function in most activities of daily living.

Monday________________________________

Tuesday________________________________

Wednesday______________________________

Thursday_______________________________

Friday_________________________________

Saturday_______________________________

Sunday_________________________________

Write in symptoms from the following list: angry, sadness, memory problems, anxious, discouraged, fearful, empty, apathetic, can't focus, making bad decisions, excessive alcohol use, racing thoughts, relaxed, abuse medications, positive, attentive, interested in life, interactive, good judgment, goal directed.

Some people find it helpful to listen to the answers of the questions of fellow travelers who have experienced trauma, tragedy, death, loss of all kinds.

Should I grieve a certain way?

There will be some common elements in the grieving journey. The way you grieve will depend on age, support system, mental health prior to the event, prior coping skills, resiliency, physical health, number of stressors, spiritual understanding, and even personality structure. Therefore, we each tend to "do the grieving journey" in our own unique way. There is not a model of how to do it that fits everyone. No one has exactly our history, our cultural heritage, our life experiences, our relationship to the trauma. In some ways, it would be easier if we all grieved in the same way. We could just copy the "scorecard" for you and track where you are in the process. It doesn't work that way. It's not so important to explain to others where you are, but it is important for you to know you have the freedom to experience grief in your own path.

❦ Some people just tell me to keep busy until the pain goes away. Is this true?

It depends on what your lifestyle was before you experienced the trauma. Some people are active and use distractions very well. Some people will use the "keep busy" approach to avoid the pain. There's no way around the grief process, you must go through the pain.

❦ Should I make decisions about moving from my house, changing jobs, developing relationships in my first year?

Nothing takes the place of having good and wise counselors around you to help you make these life-changing decisions. Find people you can trust, have your best interests in mind, and will help take care of you. Listen and respond to their advice. Readjustments after trauma can produce a need for quick decisions, but most of the time, it really doesn't. When you experience a traumatic event, give yourself time for a "professional pause" out of life to get some balance back before making decisions.

Ø They say not to be angry with God, but I can't help myself. Am I a bad person?

You have had a bad thing happen to you. No one knows how they will act toward God when they experience traumatic events. God created emotions, he created humans; and he created the ability for us to experience pain and pleasure. It's alright to yell, scream, and be angry with God; if it's not, then He's not God. The Psalms are full of raging against God about how unfair life is. This concept is not going to take God by surprise. He can handle anything a human can say or do. He expects us to not understand.

Ø If I talk about my loss, will people not want to be around me or a part of my life?

That is a true statement and a possibility with friends and family. When those who love us see us grieving, they feel helpless and powerless to stop our pain. You must talk about it, talk about it, talk about it, and talk about it some more. You can't move through the grief process except to move through it. It will overwhelm people in your life. For now, choose only those folks who can listen, understand, and validate you as a person with the right to grieve. There will be times folks can't be around you because of their own grief process. Give them the same respect that you require. It doesn't mean they love you any less. Others simply want you to move on, because they don't want to see you hurt so much.

Should I use sleeping medications or alcohol to help me cope during this period of grief?

The problem with abuse of medications or alcohol is that it doesn't speed up the grieving process. The pain goes underground, gets numbed, or at best becomes a temporary solution. In fact, more problems may develop from dependency or addictive behaviors. All medications are to be used for short-term gains and not long-term pains. There is no shortcut. When you use mood-altering drugs, you get altered not cured. This adds to the confusion and stalls the process of recovery. You may look for natural herbal remedies that some people find very helpful for them. If you experience extreme depression or anxiety or can't get adequate sleep to face decisions that must be made, then temporary relief by medications may be a valuable asset. A competent, caring, understanding professional prescriber must be involved in this decision process.

Is it possible I will never recover?

Every problem, trauma, and tragic event, produces a sense of loss for our lives. When we are out of balance, we become concerned that we can't recover. We prefer to think of it as recovering and not recovery. Let the process play out in your life. Give yourself a chance. Be realistic and rational in your expectations.

Taking in all the information you have gathered so far can produce a valuable realistic and rational expectation of yourself:

1. Your journey of grief recovery will take longer than most others think.
2. Others will have suggestions that may or may not be helpful.
3. This process will take more energy than you can imagine.
4. You will have good days and bad days in your recovery.
5. You will change during this process.
6. The grief journey will affect all areas of your life: physical, emotional, psychological, social, relational, and spiritual.
7. Your present relationships will not stay the same.
8. You will grieve for the unseen loss of your life, as well as, the seen tangible issues.
9. You will develop new coping skills for the trauma.
10. The grieving process is not a smooth journey.
11. You will surprise yourself on how well and how bad you do.
12. You will develop a new normal that will be different from anything you can imagine.
13. Issues from your past, such as, unresolved conflict will arise.
14. You will have identity confusion, as your roles in life change.
15. You will have wide emotional swings between anxiety and depression.

16. You will meet new people who will be helpful to you.
17. You will be disappointed in some friends who will not understand your process of grief.
18. You will think all of this is so unfair.
19. You may have short-term memory problems, as your brain tries to protect you from the trauma.
20. You may act socially different from your normal behavior.
21. You may feel like you are going crazy.
22. You may begin a search for meaning and purpose for your life.
23. Life will go on for your friends and family members.
24. You may break down in the strangest places.
25. You may find certain times and dates have more meaning for you.
26. You may grieve for your future.
27. Holidays may be difficult.
28. You will not have words to describe your feelings, thoughts, or behavior.

LOSS, LOSS, LOSS

It's such a four-letter word. It is a four-letter word that doesn't include hope. It is a four-letter word that is a constant and consistent companion to us all. But we don't talk about it very often, as if we would not experience it if we don't talk about it. Yet with each and every loss, the potential for a new search of you is born. The birth of insight, understanding, and refinement, all positive descriptions and words of hope come from loss.

WHAT DOES IT LOOK LIKE?

Life is a journey, and the end of the physical life is the destination. As you travel the path on the journey, you have some sense of what road you are traveling. Unfortunately, with the loss you suffered, you come to a fork in the road of your journey. At this new fork in the road of life, you are unsure of which path to take. The road you were on originally has been closed off to you, and so you are unsure of which road to take; and because of the loss of a life partner, you are now traveling alone. The recovering portion of your life is to find out how to make this new road a positive experience. Regardless, your journey of life will continue, and all the wishing in the world for the past roads will not help you.

WHAT DO WE LOOK LIKE?

The impact of grief on a person is clearly visible and manifests in several ways. The following are observable characteristics:

- Fatigue and loss of energy are so pronounced that a grief-stricken person may collapse while walking across the floor. Grief drains off energy and the desire to be physically active.

- Loss of appetite often occurs, although this is not true in all cases. Not eating, of course, adds to the loss of energy.
- The face may look ten or fifteen years older. The curve of the mouth may turn down as a manifestation of sadness, the opposite of smiling, which often cannot be expressed. The whole countenance of the person takes on an appearance of sadness. This appearance may be only temporary or may last for weeks or months
- Initially, acute grief comes in waves and much later on when grief has been overcome, a small wave of grief may appear for a moment.
- During an initial wave of grief, the person may think that he cannot breathe; and it may be so intense the person may feel he does not want to live. It is like being knocked down by an unexpected wave at the beach and having salt water get into the eyes, mouth, and nose. Wave after wave is to be expected, but the waves get smaller and the period of calm between the waves becomes longer and longer. In time, the calm prevails; but the knowledge of this wave reaction of grief can be of great benefit to the grieving person, by permitting him to know the intensity will last a short while and a less painful condition will follow.
- Another symptom of the grieving person is focusing on the lost object and talking about nothing

other than the person or thing that has been lost. (Kellerman, 1977, pp.3-4)

- A symptom of grief is to question how this has happened:

"Who am I?" and "How do I now fit into this picture called life?"
I was a husband or wife, now who am I?
I was to be a father or mother, now who am I?
I was married, now how do I fit?
I was a couple, now who am I?

The Sound of Grief
I've been busy feeding those wild horses
Again tonight
I say it's because of the stress and pace
that I fight
If you could see my pain just now, you would
see a sight
I think I am doing so well, but, you know I
can't be right
Tonight, I am running into the empty color
of the light
I want my intellect to be in control, and
it just might
But, I tell you a great truth; it's not going
to happen tonight
Brain or Heart; Who's going to win this time?
The struggle: Who am I?
The conflict: How do I fit?
Heart or Brain; Who's going to win this time?
Those fed-up wild horses are dragging my
feelings around

Hope no one calls tonight,
because I don't like
my sound
Listening to the wild horses scream
the angry words
beat me down
My internal defenses refuse to work,
really makes me
look the clown
My frozen-in-time position is a
problem that makes
the friends frown
When you are alone, you are seen as
one of the unlucky lost ones
in this town
Getting wrapped in self-explanations,
driving you in
the ground
Tending to your own desires, will start
those wild horses
to pound
Brain or Heart; Who's going to win
this time?
The struggle: Who am I?
The conflict: How do I fit?
Heart or Brain; Who's going to win
this time?
Tonight, those wild horses walking
my mind around, and are ready
to zoom
Am so out of touch with myself, just
like I am singing
out of tune

Am I doing this right or wrong?
Guess I will not learn balance
anytime soon
Hurting so bad, I am bound to spoil a
relationship, into a near
state of ruin
Need to turn my mind inside out, to
escape this tragic scene of
coming doom
I want to take me and my broken
heart, running fast up to
the moon
Passed another night, with a heavy
head, the next day
begins to loom
Brain or Heart; Who's going to win
this time?
The struggle: Who am I?
The conflict: How do I fit?
Heart or Brain; Who's going to win
this time?

Grief is not the issue from which we recover. Grief is the process that helps us recover. The purpose of grief is not to help us forget loss, but to help us grow through loss by having the courage to do the emotionally painful work.

For mourning to have a favorable outcome it appears to be necessary for a bereaved person to endure this buffeting of emotions only if he can tolerate the pining, the seemingly endless examination of how and why the loss occurred, and the anger at anyone who might have been responsible. He can gradually come

> to recognize that the loss is in truth permanent. (Bowlby, 1980, p. 93)

Why do I need to grieve? Why do I need to go through this experience? What am I learning except to feel emotional pain? What is the purpose of this event happening at this time in my life? Norman Wright explains it as grief responses express basically three things:

1. Through grief, you express your feelings about your loss and you invite others to walk with you.
2. Through grief, you express your protest at the loss, as well as, your desire to change what happened and have it not be true. This is a normal response.
3. Through grief, you express the effects you have experienced from the devastating impact of the loss. (Wright, 2004, p. 18)

For those who have experienced a traumatic loss, there is a fear of "going crazy," or others thinking I am crazy. According to the DSM-IV-TR, p.740 (the diagnostic manual for all of psychology and psychiatry) this is what "bereavement" is documented as looking like.

> This category can be used when the focus of clinical attention is a reaction to the death of a loved one. As part of their reaction to the loss, some grieving individuals present with symptoms of Major Depressive Episode (e.g., feelings of sadness and associated symptoms

such as insomnia, poor appetite, and weight loss). The bereaved individual typically regards the depressed mood as "normal," although the person may seek professional help from relief of associated symptoms such as insomnia or anorexia. The duration and expression of "normal" bereavement vary considerably among different cultural groups."

WHAT DO THEY LOOK LIKE?

Our grief is a scary and fearful thing to those who love us: our family, friends, relatives, and significant others in our lives. It becomes very clear to us that "they" don't know how to respond to us and may say or do things that we interpret as inappropriate. We need to learn about their response so we can teach them to interact with us.

- They don't know what to say to us.

  We have no models in our society to talk about loss and death in an acceptable way. Western society thrives on not talking about death. We deny its existence so we have never learned what to do or say. Our focus is recovery, not loss and death, so our language is to deny: "He passed on," "She went to the other side," "He went to become one of God's angels," "She crossed over."
- They become in touch with their own morality by being around us.

  Death means an end of us to some people. So by giving credence to death, it means to some people they will no longer exist. The death of their dreams, aspirations, and hopes of having a better life is wrapped up in having an earthly body. No one wants to be around death, and to be around us means a constant reminder that it could be us next.

- They are afraid of our intense emotions.

  One of the hardest things we can do is to be around someone who is hurting and let them hurt without doing something to ease the pain. Emotional pain will be experienced as a normal part of the grieving process. It is helpful and necessary. What is not helpful is for people in our life to say things like "Get a hold of yourself," "Be strong for the children," "Time will heal your pain," "You just can't fall apart," "Don't cry," "I know how you feel."

- They want to help us, but they feel powerless to fix the problem.

  Death of a close loved one is not an everyday experience. As our society moves farther and farther away from each other, major grief experiences occur so infrequently that we never get familiar with what the experience is like. Because of our lack of personal knowledge, we continue the habit of dealing with loss based on misinformation. We learn the problem doesn't have a solution, it must be experienced.

- They give us easy answers to complicated life struggles that don't work.

  "You have your other kids." "You can find someone else to share life with." "I am sure you will learn to live alone." "Be thankful that you have finances to make it by yourself." "The living must go on." "God will not give you more than you can handle."

- They want us to keep our faith in God.

  They tell us that we shouldn't be angry with God. We know in our rational mind that being angry with God and blaming him for our life tragedy is not the most helpful thing we can do. However, anger at God is a normal response to a life loss. We've relied on things making sense in our personal world view for all our adult life; and so when we experience loss and death, our brain spins to find a rational answer. When we can't find one, we still feel the need to assign blame. God becomes the target and a convenient place to assign blame. It becomes the one reasonable answer to place our anger. We have a need to tell someone we are angry, feeling our life has fallen apart, and not getting any answers to our questions.

WHAT DOES GOD LOOK LIKE?

As one experiences the losses in life, we must make a choice. That choice is usually found in questions: "Is God in control?" "Does God care about my loss?" "Can I trust God?" "Will God help me?"

Throughout the ages, people have tried to make some sense of these questions. Somehow, we believe that as Christians, God should never let anything, that we perceive as negative, happen to us or against us.

Scott Peck opens his renowned book *The Road Less Traveled* with three blunt truthful words, "Life is difficult." He goes on to explain that we moan more or less incessantly about the enormity of problems as if life should be easy. Life is a series of problems, of conflicts, of working out solutions, yet it is in this whole process of meeting and solving problems that life has its meaning. Problems are the cutting edge that distinguishes between success and failure.

Problems call forth our courage and wisdom; indeed, they create our courage and wisdom! It is only because of problems that we grow spiritually. When we desire to encourage the growth of the human spirit, we challenge and encourage the human capacity to solve problems. It is through the pain of confronting and resolving problems that we learn. As Benjamin Franklin said, "Those things that hurt, instruct." It is for this reason that wise people learn to deal effectively with problems." (Peck, 1978, pp. 15–16).

God Who?
I have a problem as you can see.
But I guess you have forgotten about me?
I know in my heart it's all in my head
and I try to forget as I lay in my bed.
God,
How many people are praying for me?
I am hurting as only it seems, You can see.
I'm lost and can't find a way out.
It makes me want to just scream and shout.
It appears I have developed a living Hell
but I'm not sure, it's really hard to tell.

The book of Job gives one of the most complete treatments to the issue of loss and pain. The bulk of the book centers on the issue of loss. The central theme could well be the following:

The servant of God is a man, Job, who through no fault of his own becomes an actor in the theater of loss. Job understands loss in a way that most of us will never attain.

That oath renders an instinctive judgment that life ought to be fair and that somehow God should do a better job of running the world. The world as it is versus the world as it ought to be sets up the human insecurity process to experience loss and pain. This constant tension between those two states bursts into the open in the book of Job. For three long, windy rounds, Job and his friends spar in a verbal boxing match. On the ground rules, they agree—God should reward those who do well and punish those who do evil. However, we know that it's possible to do everything right and to still be wrong.

For instance, a family of four who are coming home from a family outing and are all killed by a drunk driver. What about a young married woman with a family of small children who contracts a disease and suddenly dies?

Job, the servant of God, who is doing right and yet, experiences his world falling apart. Why is Job suffering so much apparent punishment? Job's friends, confident of God's fairness, defend the world as it is. "Job, you have sinned, you've offended God, and you're hiding a secret sin." But, Job, who knows beyond a doubt he has done nothing to deserve such punishment, cannot agree. He pleads innocent.

Gradually, however, the suffering, the consistent loss of people and possessions and the constant questioning of these endless questions, in effect, wear Job down.

He is, after all, squatting in a heap of ashes, the ruins of life. How can life be so unfair? He looks around for other examples of unfairness and sees that evil people sometimes do prosper. They don't get punished, as he would like to believe, while some godly people suffer. And, many other people live happy, fruitful lives without ever giving a thought to God" (Yancey, 1992, pp. 205–210).

At some point, just like Job, we all struggle with our losses in life and try to somehow come up with possible answers to difficult questions of our life situation.

POSSIBLE ANSWER?

God does not exist. Some Jewish writers and historians would argue, in the face of the Holocaust, this position to be true. Some people, in the face of terrible family deaths or personal tragedies, could argue this position. Why do we become so angry with someone who doesn't exist? You can't be angry with someone who doesn't exist! To feel anger toward God is healthy for humans. We don't and can't understand all the workings of God in our life. To feel something toward God is to admit that He exists. We become angry at God because we believe that He indeed exists and should have done something to stop our traumatic experience from happening. This is the process known as a spiritual journey. One in which we are all walkers toward understanding. Just maybe we don't pay attention to the fact that God does exist until things go wrong in our life. These hurts seem to focus us on the fact that life is short and we can experience pain and trauma at anytime.

> God is aware of your circumstances and moves among them. God is aware of your pain and monitors every second of it. God is aware of your emptiness and seeks to fill it in a manner beyond your dreams. Even when the situation seems out of control. Even when you are alone and afraid. God works the night shift
>
> —Ron Mehl

POSSIBLE ANSWER?

God agrees life is painful but can't do anything about it. Rabbi Harold Kushner took this approach in his best seller, *When Bad Things Happen to Good People.* After watching his son die of a terrible disease, he concluded that, "God has a hard time keeping chaos in check," and that God is a "God of justice and not of power." If God can't make my sickness go away, what good is He? God does not want you to be sick or crippled. He didn't make you to have this problem, and He doesn't want you to go on having it, but He can't make it go away. That is something which is even too hard for God. (Kushner, 1981, p.128)

Maybe we should think of things a little differently, for example, maybe we could believe that God is not the author of most suffering. It seems most suffering is created by the works of man and not so much God.

Just maybe we could think that all this human suffering does not have easy answers and the questions are hard to understand. Just maybe we could think that part of our process on earth is to experience pain and we find God in the process. Just maybe we could believe we end up doing great things for others because we first suffered through problems. Just maybe we could believe that just because we live in a certain area of the country that doesn't exempt us from traumatic events. Just maybe we could think that we don't need immediate answers to all our problems. Just maybe we could think that just because we are a good person it doesn't mean we will never suffer.

POSSIBLE ANSWER?

Life is just meaningless so don't even try to figure it out. Just go with it. In fact, one world religious view is just as good as the next one. Recently, in my counseling office, I met with parents of a third-grader who died tragically. The mother was driving their car when she swerved to avoid another car with a drunk driver. Her car slid off the road and tumbled over three or four times. Their only son was killed in the accident. Did I mention she is a third-grade teacher? Which religious worldview would you want shared with these parents if it's all the same?

Natural worldview: "Bad luck for the third-grader and the family." It doesn't mean anything any way because the survival of the species does not depend on individuals."

Atheists: "Mother should have been a better driver. Get the license of the drunk driver and prosecute to the fullest extent of the law."

Hinduism: "Hey, little boy, you are just paying for the bad karma in your previous life. Looks like you were a bad boy."

Buddhism: "There is no reason to avoid the pain of the experience; you must learn to go with it. Explore the experience of his death."

Islam: "Suffering opens up the soul and reveals it to Allah. Allah uses suffering to look within humans and tests their character, to correct the unbeliever and the believer. In Islam, suffering during one's lifetime is a way to cleanse the self of shortcomings and sins."

Christianity: "God is all powerful and He can conquer anything that challenges Him. Evil is real. Suffering is real and raises unanswerable questions from the human perspective. Suffering helps us understand our need for God. God understands pain because He experienced it in the form of Jesus Christ. Jesus introduced us to a suffering God, something the world had never seen before or since His arrival, death, burial, and resurrection. God hurts with the family of the third-grader and protects the dead boy with everlasting peace. God cares about each and every one of His creations on earth.

POSSIBLE ANSWER?

We are to walk by faith and not by sight. We have to believe that God sees and understands the beginning from the end. Even though we may not understand this side of heaven, there is a reason for our experience of loss. He is not partway or halfway in control. He is sovereign. He can do whatever He wants to do. He can control what He wants to control. He does whatever pleases Him and determines what He will and will not do. This is called the sovereignty of God. God owes no one anything. No explanations. No excuses. No help. God has no debt, no outstanding balances. No favors to return. He is absolutely independent on the control He chooses to have—in any and all situations. This makes the fact that He gives us everything of value even more astounding. Confidence in God being in control is what provides comfort for humans. His power, love, and control absolutely know no controlling force.

Understanding it is a difficult thing to do. We want to understand, and our brains spin round and round searching for an answer to life's questions. Reverend Larry Wileman is a person who has a right to have answers to life's toughest questions. He spent his whole life as an effective pastor to congregations of considerable sizes. While in the prime of his life, his car ended up under a semitractor trailer while driving on an interstate highway. The car was crushed, and Larry's body was crushed from his neck to both of his feet. I remember visiting him in the hospital and wondering how he was alive. Larry survived the car accident, the months of sitting in a wheelchair, the years of excruciating pain, the spotlight of preaching to many, to become the counselor to a few. He experiences incredible pain everyday when he leaves his house to talk with those who could never repay the debt of his encouragement. Larry grew up in a small farming community and uses that dynamic to tell a story to illustrate the idea of our trying to understand why things happen:

> There was a farmer who was totally dependent on his one horse to plow the fields and thereby his very existence to grow crops and to feed his family. One day the horse ran off from the farm. Do you think this is a good or bad thing? Most of us would think this is a bad thing because the farmer can't plow the field and can no longer provide for his family. That's our human understanding of the situation. However, it is a good thing, because the horse came back to the farm and brought several wild horses with it. Do you think this is a good or bad thing? Good thing because the farmer can sell the horses and increase his ability to provide for his family. That's our human understanding of the situation. However, this is a bad thing, because the farmer's only son and fellow field hand tried to ride one of the wild horses and fell off breaking both of his arms. Do you think this is a good or bad thing? Most of us would say this is a bad thing because it takes two people to plow the field and now the farmer is still in a bad situation. That's our human understanding of the situation. However, this was a good thing because the country was at war and all the other young men in the farming community were sent to a battle and were killed. Our human understanding would say good thing for the farmer and son. But, what about all the

> other young men of the farming community, is it a good or bad thing? We are rarely able to transcend the moment and see the bigger picture. What we consider a bad thing may be a good thing. We do not have the understanding of God in any situation.

Sometimes there will be just unexplainable questions and unknowable answers for life's traumatic suffering. That is why the Apostle Paul could write, "That is why I am suffering as I am. Yet I am not ashamed, because I know whom I have believed, and am convinced that He is able to guard what I have committed to Him against that day" (2 Tim. 1:12). If we can trust God with our eternal life, we can trust Him with our temporal problems. No problem is too small to go unnoticed by God, and no problem is too big to be outside of God's direct love or control. It is in this fact that we can take comfort. It is a good thing.

God's love is what causes Him to be with us in problems.

His grace is always sufficient. But there is even more good news. He is with us in our troubles. He does not merely send grace from heaven to meet our trials. He himself comes to help us. He says to us, "Do not be afraid…for I myself will help you" (Isa. 41:14).

In Isa. 43:2, God says, "When you pass through the waters, I will be with you; and when you pass through the rivers, they will not sweep over you. When you walk through the fire, you will not be burned; the flames will not set you ablaze." God promises specifically to be with us in our sorrows and afflictions.

He will not spare us from the waters of sorrow and the fires of adversity, but He will go through them with us.

Even when the waters and the fires are those that God himself brings into our lives, He still goes through them with us. Most of the gracious promises of God to be with us were given first to the nation of Judah during times of national spiritual decline. God, through His prophets, continually warned the people of coming judgment; yet in the midst of those warnings, we find these incredible promises of His being with them. God judged His people, but He did not forsake them. Even in their judgments, He was with them. As Isaiah said, "In all their distress He too was distressed" (Isa. 63:9).

So regardless of the nature or the cause of our adversities, God goes through them with us. He says, "I will strengthen you and help you; I will uphold you with My righteous right hand" (Isa. 41:10). It is often in the very midst of our adversities that we experience the most delightful manifestations of His love. As Paul said in 2 Cor. 1:5, "For just as the sufferings of Christ flow over into our lives, so also through Christ our comfort overflows."

God's unfailing love for us is an objective fact affirmed over and over in the Scriptures. It is true whether we believe it or not. Our doubts do not destroy God's love, nor does our faith create it. It originates in the very nature of God, who is love, and it flows to us through our union with His beloved Son.

There are doubt storms in life that we as humans live every day. You may have experienced hailstorms, snowstorms, rain storms, tornado storms, hurricanes storms; but nothing will rock your personal boat like a doubt storm. Every so often a doubt storm will roll into your life bringing a boatload of questions that can't be answered with three verses and a prayer. These storms will bring fear and questions that can't be answered this side of eternity. Sometimes the doubt storm will come in the form of your personal physical health, your mental health, your relational health, or your spiritual health. You find yourself asking, "Why me, Lord?" All you seem to get is more questions than answers.

Sometime the doubt storm will come from your work or career that isn't as fulfilling as you had hoped it would be. You find yourself asking, "Where did I miss what I was going to do that would make me happy, Lord?" All you get is more questions than answers.

Sometimes the doubt storm comes when you open your eyes to the hurt and pain in the world. You find yourself asking, "If God is in control, why are so many good and godly people suffering so much pain?" All you get is more questions than answers.

We will almost always struggle with doubts about God's love during our times of adversity. If we never had to struggle, our faith would not grow. But the experience of that love and the comfort it is intended to bring is dependent upon our believing the truth about God's love as it is revealed to us in the Scriptures. Doubts about God's love, allowed to harbor in our hearts, will surely deprive us of the comfort of His love.

But we must engage in the struggle with our doubts; we must not let them overwhelm us. During seemingly intolerable times, we must remember that Got is in control.

Because He is in control, we can experience comfort. Nothing takes God by surprise. His love is infinite, but if His power is finite then we can't trust Him completely.

The problem with understanding God's control is that it frequently doesn't appear God is in control of the circumstances of life. Good, solid Christians suffer consequences beyond their control. We suffer due to other's mistakes and failures.

The Bible is very specific about God's control. No one can act and no circumstances can occur outside the bounds of God's will. God does as He pleases, comforts whom He pleases, and no one can change His plan or change His direction.

"Our God is in Heaven; He does whatever pleases Him" (Ps. 115:3).

"For the Lord Almighty has proposed, and who can thwart Him? His hand is stretched out, and who can turn it back?" (Isa. 14:27).

"I make known the end from the beginning, from ancient times, what is still to come. I say: my purpose will stand, and I will do all that I please" (Isa. 46:10).

"In Him we were also chosen, having been predestined according to the plan of Him who works out everything in conformity with the purpose of His will" (Eph. 1:11).

If God is in control, then He can provide comfort for us when we are in need. God has a purpose and a plan for our life and has the power to carry out the plan. Because we know God is in control, we can trust Him through the conflicts of life. He is directly involved in our life and committed to work with us through the pain we experience.

Dr. James Dobson has written a book called *When God Doesn't Make Sense.* He proposes that it is an incorrect scriptural view to say that we will always comprehend what God is doing and how our loss and pain fit into his plan.

"Also tell me, where did we get the notion that the Christian life is a piece of cake? Where is the evidence for the "name it, claim it" theology that promises God will skip along in front of us with his great cosmic broom, sweeping aside each trial and every troubling uncertainty? To the contrary, Jesus told his disciples that they should anticipate suffering. He said, "I have told you these things, so that in me you may have peace. In this world you will have trouble. But take heart! I have overcome the world" (John 16:33). Paul wrote, "In all our troubles my joy knows no bounds. For when we came into Macedonia, this body of ours had not rest, but we were harassed at every turn—conflicts on the outside, fears within" (2 Cor. 7:4–5). Peter left no doubt about difficulties in this Christian life when he wrote, "Dear friends, do not be surprised at the painful trial you are suffering, as though something strange were happening to you. But rejoice that you participate in the sufferings of Christ, so that you may be overjoyed when his glory is revealed" (1 Pet. 4:12–13). Note in each of these references the coexistence of both joy and pain.

My concern is that many believers apparently feel God owes them smooth sailing or at least a full explanation (and perhaps an apology) for the hardships they encounter. We must never forget that he, after all, is God. He is majestic and holy and sovereign. He is accountable to no one.

He is not an errand boy who chases the assignments we dole out. He is not a genie who pops out of the bottle to satisfy our whims. He is not our servant, we are his. And our reason for existence is to glorify and honor him. Even so, sometimes he performs mighty miracles on our behalf. Sometimes he chooses to explain his action in our lives. Sometimes his presence is as real as if we had encountered him face to face. But at other times when nothing makes sense—when what we are going through is "not fair," when we feel all alone in God's waiting room—he simply says, trust me.

Does this mean that we are destined to be depressed and victimized by the circumstances of our lives? Certainly not. Paul said we are "more than conquerors." He wrote in Phil. 4:4–7:

"Rejoice in the Lord always. I will say it again: Rejoice! Let your gentleness be evident to all. The Lord is near. Do not be anxious about anything, but in everything, by prayer and petition, with thanksgiving, present your requests to God. And the peace of God, which transcends all understanding, will guard your hearts and your minds in Christ Jesus."

Clearly, what we have in Scripture is a paradox. On the one hand, we are told to expect suffering and hardship that could even cost us our lives. On the other hand, we are encouraged to be joyful, thankful, and "of good cheer." How do those contradictory ideas link together? How can we be triumphant and under intense pressure at the same time? How can we be secure when surrounded by insecurity?

That is a mystery which, according to Paul, "transcends all understanding".

Truth number one, God is active and present in our lives at all times.

Human perception sometimes poses questions the mind is incapable of answering. But valid answers always exist. For those of us who are followers of Jesus Christ, it just makes good sense not to depend too heavily on our ability to make the pieces fit—especially when we're trying to figure out the Almighty!

Not only is human perception a highly flawed and imprecise instrument, but our emotions are even less reliable. No, we can't depend on our feelings and passions to govern our lives or to assess the world around us. Emotions are unreliable, biased wild horses. They lie as often as they tell the truth. They are manipulated by hormones, especially in the teen years; and they wobble dramatically from early morning, when we're rested, to the evening, when we're tired. One of the evidences of emotional maturity is the ability (and the willingness) to overrule feelings and govern our behavior with the intellect and the will.

If perceptions or emotions are suspect at best, then we must be extremely wary in accepting what they tell us about God. Unfortunately, many believers seem unaware of this source of confusion and disillusionment.

It is typical for vulnerable people to accept what they "feel" about the Lord at face value. But what they feel may reflect nothing more than a momentary frame of mind. Furthermore, the mind, the body, and the spirit are very close neighbors. One usually catches the ills of the next. If a person is depressed, for example, it affects not only his emotional and physical well-being, his spiritual life suffers too. He may conclude, "God doesn't love me. I just don't feel his approval." Likewise, the first thing an individual is likely to say when diagnosed with a threatening physical illness is, "Why would God do this to me?" These three faculties are inextricably linked, and they weaken the objectivity of our perception.

This understanding becomes extremely important when it comes to evaluation of our relationship with God. Even when he seems one thousand miles away and uninterested in our affairs, he is close enough to touch. A wonderful illustration of his unseen presence is described in Luke 24, verses 13 and 14, when two of Jesus' disciples were walking toward a village called Emmaus, about seven miles from Jerusalem. They had seen their Master horribly crucified three days earlier, and they were severely depressed. Everything that they hoped for had died on that Roman cross. All the dramatic things Jesus had said and done now appeared contrived and untrue. He had spoken with such authority, but now he was dead and laid to rest in a borrowed tomb. He claimed to be the Son of God, yet they had heard him cry in his last hours, "My God, My God, why have you forsaken me?" (Matt. 27:46). The disciples couldn't have been more confused. What was the meaning of the time they had spent with this man who called himself the Messiah?

What they didn't realize was that Jesus was walking that dusty road with them at that very moment, and that they were about to be given the greatest news ever heard by human ears. It would revolutionize their lives and turn the rest of the world upside down. At the time, however, all they saw were facts that could not be harmonized.

If you find yourself on that dusty road to Emmaus today, and the circumstances in your life have left you confused and depressed, I have a word of counsel for you. Never assume God's silence or apparent inactivity is evidence of his disinterest. Let me say it again. Feelings about his inaccessibility mean nothing! Absolutely nothing! His Word is infinitely more reliable than our spooky emotions. Rev. Reubin Welch, minister and author, once said, "With God, even when nothing is happening—something is happening." It is true. The Lord is at work in His own unique way even when our prayers seem to echo back from an empty universe.

Truth number two, God does not function on our time schedule. One of the greatest destroyers of faith is timing that doesn't fit our preconceived notions. We live in a fast-paced world where we have come to expect instant responses to every desire and need—instant coffee, instant potatoes, instant cash from the little money machine, instant relief for sore muscles and minor backache. It's almost our birthright to make the world jump at our demands. But God doesn't operate that way. He is never in a hurry. And sometimes, He can be agonizingly slow in solving the problems we bring to his attention. It's almost enough to make an impatient believer give up and try something else.

Before bailing out, however, we should take another look at the story of Mary, Martha, and their brother, Lazarus, as told in John 11. The members of this little family were among Jesus' closest friends during the time of his earthly ministry.

Verse 5 says, "Jesus loved Martha and her sister and Lazarus." It was reasonable, given this affection, for them to expect certain favors from Jesus, especially if life-threatening emergencies ever occurred. Indeed, they were soon confronted by precisely that situation when Lazarus became desperately ill.

His sisters did the logical thing—they sent an urgent note to Jesus, saying, "Lord, the one you love is sick" (v. 3). They had every reason to believe He would respond.

Mary and Martha waited and watched the road for Jesus' appearance, but He did not come. Hours dragged into anxious days with no sign of the Master. Meanwhile, Lazarus was steadily losing ground. He was obviously dying. But where in the world was Jesus? Did He get the message? Didn't He know the seriousness of the illness? Didn't He care? As the sisters sat vigilantly at his bedside, Lazarus soon closed his eyes in death.

The sisters were grief stricken. Also, they must have been extremely frustrated with Jesus. He was out there somewhere performing miracles for total strangers, opening blind eyes and healing the lame. Yet here they were in critical need of His care, and He was too busy to come. I can imagine Mary and Martha saying quietly to each other, "I just don't understand. I thought He loved us. Why would He abandon us like this?" They wrapped Lazarus in grave clothes and conducted a sad little funeral. Jesus did not attend. Then they said good-bye to their brother and lovingly placed his body in a tomb.

Mary and Martha loved Jesus will all their hearts, but it would have been reasonable for them to have been annoyed when He showed up four days later. They may have been tempted to say, "Where have you been, sir? We tried to tell you that your friend was dying, but we couldn't get your attention. Well, you're too late now. You could have saved him, but apparently there were more important things on your mind." Mary's actual words were much more respectful, of course. What she said was, "Lord,…if you had been here, my brother would not have died" (John 11:21). She wept as she spoke and the Lord was "deeply moved in spirit and troubled" (v. 33).

Jesus then performed one of His most dramatic miracles as He called Lazarus out of the tomb.

You see, the master was not really late at all. He only appeared to be overdue.

He arrived at the precise moment necessary to fulfill the purposes of God—just as He always does.

With no disrespect intended, let me say that what happened there in Bethany is characteristic of the Christian life.

Haven't you noticed that Jesus usually shows up about four days late? He often arrives after we have wept and worried and paced the floor—after we have sweated out the medical examination or fretted our way through business reverses. If He had arrived on time, we could have avoided much of the stress that occurred in His absence. Yet it is extremely important to recognize that He is never actually late. God's economy of time and energy is very different from ours. Most of us in western nations are motivated to use every second of our existence for some gainful purpose. But the Lord sometimes permits our years to be "squandered," or so it would seem, without a backward glance.

What conclusions can we draw from these seeming contradictions, except to "let God be God?" He does not explain himself to man. We can say with confidence that while His purposes and plans are very different from ours, He is infinitely just and His timing is always perfect. He intervenes at just the right moment for our ultimate good. Until we hear from Him, then, we would be wise not to get in a hurry.

Truth number three, God is in love with human beings.

One of the most breathtaking concepts in all of Scriptures is the revelation that God knows each of us personally, and that we are on His mind both day and night. There is simply no way to comprehend the full implications of this love by the King of kings and Lord of lords. He is all-powerful and all-knowing, majestic and holy, from everlasting to everlasting. Why would he care about us—about our needs, our welfare, our fears? We have been discussing situations in which God doesn't make sense. His concern for us mere mortals is the most inexplicable of all.

Job also had difficulty understanding why the Creator would be interested in human beings. He asked, "What is man that you make so much of him, that you give him so much attention, that you examine him every morning?" (Job 7:17–18). (Dobson pp.40–59)

DEFINING NORMAL

A thirty-six-year-old man is tragically left with two young children when his wife dies suddenly in a car wreck. After a few months of intense shock, he tells friends, "I just want to be normal!"

In early 1995, a huge blast rips apart a federal building in downtown Oklahoma City. The blast annihilated the day-care center in the heart of the building. Precious babies from the day-care center were killed. Oklahoma would never be normal again in the way it saw terrorism. The people who lost friends, relatives, and coworkers would not be normal ever again.

Normal is that state of being which guides, controls, or regulates proper or acceptable behavior and emotions. We hardly ever function in the normal range.

So asking to be normal after a tragic personal calamity is making the wrong statement.

Grief Song
Grief will shock your life,
Sap your will to live,
Cut your heart like it didn't exist,
Laugh in your face.

Tell you lies in the mirror,
Parade around in your tortured mind.
An uninvited monster within,
For grief doesn't care who or whom it hurts.
It eats up everything in sight,
Who knows your weaknesses, and kills your
strengths.
Normal is nowhere to be found.

℘ Normal means that you will experience shock.

God has created a wonderful complex organism that works in instrumental perfection. At the time of a traumatic incident, the mind may shut down to protect the person from further trauma. This is why people can look "put together" when they have just experienced a horrible incident. The mind flips into a survival mode to let the person do what is necessary for daily survival. This automatic reflex reaction is something God has given us to use in situations. There seems to be a loss of emotional connection within the person and the outside world. The person might later say they felt like an outsider observing the situation. They may also feel like an actor in this tragic play. The person distances from others, feeling out of control, fearful, and searching for protection. The person may have inappropriate emotions like laughing at the funeral service or crying over seemingly trivial things. The person's shock acceptance may cause others to think "he's doing so well!" This stage can last from minutes to months and can reoccur if the person continues to feel out of control. Because this is not a normal situation for the person, the individual is constantly rehearsing the details of who, what, where, when and why. The mind is doing everything necessary to try to provide a normal answer to an extremely abnormal situation. The brain finds, of course, that no answer seems to satisfy in this stage.

Shock is a temporary escape from reality. As long as it is temporary, then it will have served the purpose for which God intended it. But if the person continues in the shock state, it leads to very unhealthy behaviors.

If I die today who will know?
My Self died today,
shock, disbelief, depression, anxiety…
My Self died today,
no feelings, too much feelings, emptiness...
My Self died today,
no tears, too many tears...
My Self died today,
overwhelming floods of emotional pain...
My Self died today,
no friends, too many friends...
My Self died today,
When I saw you lying there…

Normal means you will experience denial.

The husband and wife of fourteen years had a very satisfying relationship. As his life progressed, he developed heart problems. A surgery was scheduled to reopen a blocked artery. The surgery seemed to go pretty well. The wife went home after her husband left surgery and was in the recovery room. She no sooner got home when the hospital called to tell her of surgical complications. She rushed back to the hospital to realize her greatest fear, for her husband had died. Several months later, she complained to her pastor how unfairly she had been treated by the hospital. She stated they were unconcerned and uncaring about her feelings and needs. The pastor gently broke through her denial system by helping her see the hospital is not the issue, the problem is her husband had died.

Denial is the state of refusing to admit to the harsh reality of truth. It is the constant assertion that something terrible could not happen to you and in fact, did not happen to you. "Because I am a child of God, He would not allow me to face awful consequences," is often the thinking process. Dr. Mortan Bard has described denial as a "means of resting while working through an emotional trauma." "Sometimes the person will be able to feel and work on the painful emotions aroused by the experience; at other times, he or she will defend against the feelings by denying them. This process has been described as a waxing and waning of tension and has been compared to the natural pattern of sleeping and waking."

Denial may be very practical as a person comes face to face with loss. The loss may be physical such

> as loss of limb, loss of activity, loss of appearance, or loss of memory. The loss could be material such as loss of possessions, loss of finances, loss of property, or loss of home. The intangible losses are the ones that seem to affect people the most and are subconscious; such as loss of love, loss of faith, loss of trust, loss of hope, loss of identity, loss of time, loss of talent, loss of past, present, or future, and loss of role. There is just so much emotional energy available in the body and mind. If the energy is used to work through the painful emotions and acceptance of the reality of the loss, little is left over for other activities. Those who become easily drained of energy are those who are using denial to protect themselves from their own trauma.

When denial is used as avoidance, other aspects of a person's life may become unimportant. They may avoid work, avoid relationships, avoiding taking care of themselves. They may avoid the grieving process and begin focusing on a project. People must grieve for their losses to get through the denial state. Each loss brings up old baggage that we carry along through our other life experiences. Because we are meant to be survivors, we have been able to "push down" our negative experiences. In other words, denial has been very good to us. However, when we get overloaded, we must work through the denial by mourning our losses. Losses such as these:

Loss of loved ones
Loss of basic beliefs
Loss of faith in God
Loss of control over present, or future
Loss of objects
Loss of power
Loss of mental health
Loss of a sense of justice and fairness
Loss of trust in others
Loss of physical health

Normal means you will experience anger.

The parents of a beautiful teenage girl had prayed daily for her growth physically, spiritually, and socially. They were careful to lead a life of godly devotion. They had a safe middle-class existence, for which they thanked God. One night, their daughter did not come home. The hospital emergency room doctor explained to them a terrible car accident had taken the life of their precious daughter. The shaken parents spent years in their anger toward God. They asked "Didn't we love God? Didn't we ask God to protect our daughter? Didn't we live godly lives? How could God let our daughter die?"

Anger is the emotion that exposes unfairness. It is expressed as the hope for finding an explanation or justification for something to be the way it is. You may be angry over the following:

Angry over the way the person left you
Angry with all the details that must now be completed while you are alone
Angry with the financial state in which you find yourself
Angry with the loss of control you now feel
Angry that the rest of the world goes on and doesn't stop to see your pain
Angry with others for going on with their lives
Angry with how you see your life turning out
Angry with the role changes you didn't ask for
Angry that you are so lonely
Angry with God

It is often expressed as, "If I am a Christian, how can I be so angry with God?"

Angry Words
Thinking and expecting way too much.
Wanting the experience of human touch.
Badly needing someone to hold,
Emotionally naked when self-esteem is sold.
Do you think I'm asking for too much?
Having the need to be the great pretender,
Knowing appropriate honesty is hard to render.
Under the mask is covered with war paint,
Wearing the anger, it's hard to find the saint.
Do you think I'm asking?
In the end it's surrender every day,
When reality takes a life and just strips it away.
Producing the illusion of being a bargain,

Trying hard to reconnect the brain and heart,
again.
Do you think I'm?
Sadly, not expecting any miracles around here,
Being one step away from understanding, or
fear?
Love is dangerous because of risking the pain,
They ask what part of the hard heart remains.
Do you think?
Now, down to the heart of the matter,
Having no one to feel is sadder and sadder.
All the answers don't amount to much,
When the need is a little human touch.
Do you think I'm asking for too much?

Anger is very normal for every human, and even the most godly person can well feel angry, even though trying hard to sublimate this feeling. After all, we are human and need to feel free to express our anger to God. He is big enough to handle our displaced anger. It is a normal part of the grieving process. Any emotional pain drains your energy by creating a negative feeling that has to be resolved. The human reaction is to redirect the negative feelings outside of you, to externalize them, at whatever is perceived to have caused the pain. No matter what a person says, they feel that God is to blame for their pain.

By telling God you are angry, you can begin to allow the emotional wound to heal. If any loss is to heal in the fullest way, the anger it generates must be expressed. To hold in anger only multiplies the pain. God has given us the outlet to express emotional pain.

Problems occur when people do not express their anger but trap it inside.

- Normal means you will experience depression.

  "I have served the Lord all my life," stated the older Christian man. "I have prayed for my daughter and her family for years. How could God not protect her? How could God let her die so suddenly? Where was God when she got that fatal disease? I feel utter despair!" Eventually in the grief process, the feelings of utter despair come and seem to cloak us like a London fog. It is as if God has turned away from us. It is as if He no longer hears and responds to our heartfelt prayers. It's impossible to believe that God is with us following any significant loss. To understand depression, you need to note the situation and the feelings involved. Is the sadness appropriate given the loss? If the depression fits the loss, then let it be, for now.

Have you read some of David's psalms recently?

"Why art thou cast down, oh my soul?" (Ps. 42:5).

"O my God, my soul is cast down within me," (Ps. 42:6).

"Why art thou cast down? Hope in God; for I shall yet praise Him, who is the health of my countenance," (Ps. 43:5).

Or listened to Elijah?

"O Lord, take away my life," (1 Kings 19:4).

Or Jonah?

"It is better for me to die than to live," (Jon. 4:3).

Or heard Jesus' words in the garden as He was in pain and in prayer?

"My soul is exceeding sorrowful, even unto death," (Matt. 26:38).

Can you find better descriptions of depression—a depression in which the person almost despaired of life itself? Many of the depressive Psalms speak of the countenance, the person's face, and how accurate those Psalms are! The person who is depressed and dejected has a miserable countenance. He looks troubled, worried, unhappy, as if he is bearing the weight of the world on his shoulders.

Another very common symptom of depression is tears. "My tears have been my meat day and night," (Ps. 42:3), says the psalmist. This is an amazingly accurate psychological statement! Depression often brings a loss of appetite. You just don't feel like eating. Because food seems repulsive, you begin to live on tears instead of food. "My tears have been my meat," and some of us could add, "Yes, and my vegetable, salad, dessert, and drink too." What's wrong? Unable to stop crying, you feed on despair, and that of course increases the depression.

Before a person can deal with depression, he must acknowledge it. And many a Christian, if he were completely honest about his emotions, would have to admit: "Yes, depression is an acquaintance of mine too. I know what you are talking about."

By denying their depression, many Christians add to their troubles. They add guilt on top of the depression and thereby double the problem. Let's say that a severe depression is equal to carrying one ton of emotional weight. That's about what it feels like, isn't it?

To carry a ton on your back is bad, but you may have the strength for it. However, when you then add guilt by saying, "There's something wrong with me, because I have this depression," you have then doubled the weight; and that's an impossible load for anyone to carry.

Depression is not necessarily a sign of spiritual failure. In the Scripture stories, some of the greatest depressions came as emotional letdowns following the greatest spiritual successes. This was true in the life of Elijah. After that greatest moment in his life, the triumph over the prophets of Baal on Mt. Carmel, what happened? The next time we see him, he is sitting alone under the juniper tree asking God to take his life. Abraham had a similar experience (Gen. 15). And many of us have too. Depression seems to be nature's emotional kickback. It is a reaction like the wallop from firing a gun of heavy caliber. It is nature's recoil, or perhaps the balance wheel in what C.S. Lewis calls "the law of undulation" in the human personality.

Unfortunately, some of our Christian friends can be our worst enemies at this point, offering us false and unrealistic advice. There are Christians who have little understanding about depression. Because their own personalities are not very subject to it, they fail to understand people who suffer depression. This can be especially cruel when two such people are married to one another. If a husband does not suffer much from depression but his wife does, he may have a difficult time appreciating her emotions and her moods. It can be a doubly cruel situation if he uses her depressed time to put a spiritual heavy on her.

You can't assume that because you never suffer from depression, you are therefore more spiritual. C.S. Lewis once said that about half the times when we credit ourselves with virtue, it's really just a matter of temperament and constitution, and not of spirituality. (Collins, 1977, pp. 112–115)

How God responds to us when we are depressed is important. He accepts us and will respond to us. We can cry out and He understands. In six verses in John 10:33-38, it states three times that Jesus wept. Jesus did the painful work of grief.

What we must keep in perspective is depression will not last forever. Of course, the person in this state is convinced he will remain here all his days. Any attempt to convince him otherwise doesn't seem to work. However, the experience of countless others has proven you will move through this stage.

- Normal means you will feel guilt.

  "God, why did you let me survive the accident? It makes more since for you to have let my spouse live. They are more capable of taking care of these responsibilities than I am. I am nothing compared to them." Guilt is the feeling of being unworthy. It is the questioning of God that He made a mistake. Guilt can so hold a person as to direct energy inward to punish oneself for even being alive! This kind of guilt takes on non-logical and uncontrollable behaviors. It selects negative memory recollections to punish oneself for every wrongdoing. It tries to blame self for the loss.

Severe guilt becomes an all-consuming trap. It is a self-fulfilling prophecy that you are the secretly evil and bad person you have always felt you were. For example, when someone significant dies, we feel guilty about some of the things we said to them, things we did or did not do for them, and the many times we hurt them. We may even blame ourselves for their death. Because we believe we have sinned against them, we ought and should feel guilty. Since they died, we reason, we can never be forgiven for that sin. Well, this is why God invented grace.

Grace is defined as unmerited mercy and favor. It can't be earned, bought, or repaid. The failure of "accepting what can't be changed" drives many Christians to wallow in the pit of guilt. When you admit guilt and see it as irrational, you have a chance to move onward.

"Thirteen-Minute Cry"

"My father was involved in a tragic accident. He had some men working at his home on a defective furnace. In the course of the morning, he decided to go to town to buy a newspaper. He always joked that he had to read the newspaper daily to see if he was in the obituary. This morning was no different.

He started his truck and then decided to get out and tell the workmen where he was going. The truck kicked into reverse, or possibly he didn't have the gearshift totally engaged in park. We'll never know exactly what happened. The result was that his truck backed up as he was standing at the rear of it. It pinned him against an electrical pole and crushed his hip.

Living in a rural area in southeast Georgia and in a very small town, it took a while for the ambulance to arrive. His pastor, who was also his cousin, went promptly to the scene. My dad told him, "I need the Master's help." And then he asked the pastor to pray for a cousin who was soon to have his leg amputated due to a blood disease.

I had started a new job just a few months prior to the accident. I was called to the front desk of the business and given the news. I promptly called the hospital and spoke with my dad.

The next day after surgery I spoke to him again. During this conversation I heard him laughing and joking with the nurses in the background. He had to end the phone call but asked, "Can you call me back in thirty minutes?"

I never spoke to him again. He was put into the Intensive Care Unit and was being monitored for his heart but the doctors insisted the outlook was good. We were quite surprised when he died two days later of a massive heart attack.

His wife told me just that morning that she did not plan to go to the hospital that day since he was doing so well. By the time I came home at lunch, there was a message on my answering machine. With certain surety of the news, I made the call that would change my life. I wailed when I heard the news that he had died. I walked the length of my living room floor and wailed.

Of course, I only had a short amount of time away from work to attend the funeral, only a week. When I returned to the workplace, it was business as usual.

Ironically, I had been telling my dad that I would fly down to see him. Having never flown in an airplane, it was a big step for me when my husband and I did indeed fly to Georgia to see my dad one last time.

In our modern times, when can a person grieve? How can a woman who works full time and cares for a family take the time to fully part with her father?

I learned that when a parent dies, no one else on earth gives or replaces the love that a parent imparts to you. You may have meaningful relationships, very fulfilling friendships, but no one else on earth will ever love you quite like a parent.

My dad was my encourager. When the world knocked me down, he was there to tell a joke and lift me up. I often felt his humor was born of pain and struggles he'd had in his own life. He had taught me as a child to love the Lord, exalt Him in all things, and worship Him with a willing heart. He had laid the spiritual foundation, smooth and solid as a rock, which I rely upon today.

But I had a hard time letting go because I had no time, and no place to grieve. I was 1,700 miles from his family and could not visit his grave. I had to return to work full-time while caring for my family, and I was very sad inside.

One morning soon after his death, I was short-tempered with a coworker in the break room at work. I wasn't angry with the young man; I was in emotional turmoil. During the morning break, I got into my car and drove into the country. During the drive, I released the pent up tears, which I'd had to hold inside while at work. It was a thirteen-minute cry. I returned to the workplace and resumed taking calls for technical support. I also apologized to the young coworker for my rudeness and explained that I was missing my father. He said he understood.

That spring I had more thirteen minute cries. A short drive into the country and back into town on my breaks or lunch hour allowed me to shed the needed tears. I have a theory about grieving; it is that we humans do not deal well with death because we were never created to feel it physically or emotionally. It was not in God's master plan.

While I will always miss my dad, I understand that he did his job well when he laid the foundation for me to be happy. He introduced me to our heavenly Father. The spiritual foundation he paved has led to a strong Christian life with my family. His example of encouraging and humor are two gifts I will never forget, and that I will in turn pass on to my children and if I am so blessed, in generations to come."

Author: LaRose Karr

❧ Normal means you will have unanswered questions.

When you are not able to give any rational explanations for your loss, then your brain continues to spin to find answers. When something doesn't make sense you will continue to mull over the facts, all possible situations where you believe you could have done something differently. Often there are no answers for your experience. Here are some of the questions with which recovering individuals struggle:

Why did this happen? We ask this because of our expectations of how life is to unfold. When expectations don't meet reality then we have an unanswered question. Trying to answer the question of "why" is an important part of acceptance of the loss. Sometimes the greater the distance between expectations of life, and the reality of the loss tends to predict how difficult it will be to reconcile or accept your loss.

Why can't I get moving forward? You have lost control over your life because of your loss, and so moving forward is an individual accomplishment. Your physical body has been affected. Your brain has experienced a trauma. You don't feel like doing anything. Don't wait until you feel like something because it is irrational to think that you will feel like moving forward for some period of time. Most people have to do something, and then the feeling will come later. Doing something is better than doing nothing, even though you will find it difficult. Focus on the concept of making a small but reasonable change on a daily basis and call that success.

When do I go back to work? This means you are appropriately worried about what others will say and do in your presence in the work environment. Most people do not have the ability to stay out of work for an extended period. As soon as you think you can go back to work and be productive, on some level, you should try to go back to work. Most people say they feel better when they can see themselves as being productive at work. This presents a positive and a real distraction to thinking about something other than your loss.

How do I deal with my loneliness? Feeling of being alone meets the reality that you are alone. Even when surrounded by those who love you, you still feel alone with your loss. Targeting both your thoughts and behavior is especially important in this stage. Some individuals end up making bad choices and decisions because of loneliness. Establishing new relationships can be especially tempting during this time period. New relationships that can be damaging once you are farther along in the recovery process. One needs to target the loneliness by continuing to be with those whom you have established long-term relationships and not new "bad decision" relationships.

What's my story now? Keep in mind that you have a story to tell others about who you are, who you have been, and who you can become. It's important to be reminded of this fact.

YOUR STORY

If your story until now was going to be published in book form, what would its title be?

If your story built up to a major achievement you have made, what would that be?

If your story was an epic, what noble cause have you been championing?

What was the motivation behind your accomplishments?

What remains to be done?

Describe a scene in your story in which you, the main character, faced a major setback that brought out the best in you. What characteristics or personal quality did this reveal?

What other setbacks did you face, and what did you learn from them?

What events in your story foreshadow what lies ahead for you?

What parts of your story do you want to leave out in the second half of life?

Who have been the most important people in your story thus far, and what role will they play in the rest of your story?

Normal means you will have a choice.

> As we go about defining the new normal we move through shock, denial, anger, depression, and guilt. In order to grieve fully, we must choose to grieve. Sometimes it is picking the place and times of grief. Sometimes we just become overwhelmed with grief. But we must choose to recover. To not choose is making a choice not to recover from grief. It is to choose to not redefine normal, to be stuck.

To choose is to do the work of acceptance. *The Grief Recovery Book* has been a major help to those who come across its path. In the book, the authors recall their own traumatic events, and then the search for acceptance that's a part of recovery. My search for acceptance has been and continues to be quite a journey. This journey reminds me that my happiness is an inside job. My happiness depends on the choice within me to not fight the changes beyond my control. My happiness depends on my willingness to accept these changes. The secret is to remember that happiness only comes when I accept that which just seems impossible to accept. I don't need to accept it for the rest of my life, just for today. As a direct result of all I've lost and all I've accepted, I've become a new person. My reactions are different. I'm more aware. Losses have caused the greatest changes in my life. The greater the loss equals the greater the change. Changes scare me. I have consistently needed a better understanding of myself to accept changes. (James, 1988, pp.132, 133)

The Pain Keeps Coming

Here it comes again…
If I could only escape you for a minute,
They say the minutes will get longer.
Pain, pain…Go away. Come again another day.
Now I can stand you for an hour.
Here it comes again…
If I could only escape you for an hour.
I made an hour but now it's only minutes.
Pain, pain…go away. Come again another day.
I ran from you for a day this time.
Here it comes again…
Minute. Hour. Day.
The choices are too many to overcome the
pain.
Pain, pain…go away. Come again another day.
Here it comes again….
Minute. Hour. Day. Year.
Pain, pain…Go away. Come again another day.
Pain, pain…Go away. Come again another day.
Pain, pain. Go away. Come again another
day…
I choose another day…

Jesus forced people to choose. He forced His disciples, the rich young ruler, and anyone He contacted to choose.

So now choose!

Jesus was headed through Jericho on His way to celebrate the Passover in Jerusalem. Jericho is north and east of Jerusalem. It is an international crossroad located where the main routes north, south, east, and west all came together. The customs house there, where taxes were collected, was a busy place. Zaccheus was the tax collector in charge of the Jericho customs house. The great teacher, Jesus, was headed there just ahead of the crowd of people. Zaccheus had heard much about this celebrity and he wanted to do anything to see him. So he climbed up a tree, got out on the limb, and hung over the road (Luke 19:4). As Jesus approached the tree, He stopped and in the middle of the hundreds of people, He picked Zaccheus out and said, "Come down out of that tree because I'm staying at your house."

Zaccheus had a choice!

We human beings, we constantly make choices. An animal's search for food or the care it must take of its young is pretty much programmed into the animal so that it acts without having to make a decision. But you and I, because we can exercise our free will, are able to make choices between one course of action and another; and because of this, we can get caught between opposing desires.

One of the most telling examples of making choices is the situation explained at the beginning of Jesus' ministry. The beginning is presented in Matt. 19, the starting discourse and encounter with the rich young ruler (vv. 16–22).

The rich, young ruler felt he knew the answers to "Who am I?" and "How do I fit in?" and he answered both of these questions by not dealing with the choice that Jesus presented. Jesus knew the young man was missing an important quality. Jesus knew he was utterly lacking a sense of his own sinfulness. His desire for salvation was to do away with the conflict of anxiety and frustration but not in committing himself to Christ (Matt. 19:22).

The conflict of giving away his possessions meant more to him than giving himself to Christ. Since material things were more important to him, he could not come to Jesus if it meant giving up his things. His self-concept and self-esteem were tied up in his possessions. "Who am I?" I am rich, I am young, I am in control of my life. "How do I fit in?" I am prominent. I am secure in knowing my standing in life. I am powerful. I am influential. My self-esteem is what others think of me.

To choose to define the new normal is to choose recovery in the grief process. The new normal is emotional energy returning, balanced activities, suffering lessons, regaining sense of trust, and a new appreciation of life. All these areas come as a result of searching. Because searching leads to acceptance. Therese Rando, in her book *Grieving: How to Go On Living When Someone You Love Dies* has developed a scale to suggest that you need to be able to track changes in yourself, in your relationship with what you lose, and in your relationship with others. As you review and score the following scales, the conclusions you reach will help you decide if you are moving toward a new normal. On a scale of 1–10 (1 meaning no recovery and 10 meaning total recovery) rate yourself as of today in response to each question.

CHANGES IN MYSELF BECAUSE OF MY LOSS

1. I have returned to my normal levels of functioning in most areas of life. _____
2. My overall symptoms of grief have declined. _____
3. My feelings do not overwhelm me when I think about my loss or someone mentions it. _____
4. Most of the time I feel all right about myself. _____
5. I enjoy myself and what I experience without feeling guilty. _____
6. My anger has diminished, and when it occurs, it is handled appropriately. _____
7. I don't avoid thinking about things that could be or are painful. _____
8. My hurt has diminished and I understand it. _____
9. I have completed what I need to do about my loss. _____
10. I can think of positive things. _____
11. My pain does not dominate my thoughts. _____
12. I can handle special days or dates without being totally overwhelmed by memories. _____
13. I can remember the loss on occasion without pain and without crying. _____
14. There is meaning and significance to my life. _____
15. I am able to ask the question "How?" rather than "Why?" at this time._____

16. I see hope and purpose in life, in spite of my loss. _____
17. I have energy and can feel relaxed during the day. _____
18. I no longer fight the fact that the loss has occurred. _____
19. I am learning to be more comfortable with my new identity and being without what I lost. _____
20. I understand that my feelings over the loss will return periodically, and I can accept that. _____
21. I understand what grief means and have a greater appreciation for it. _____

CHANGES IN MY RELATIONSHIP WITH THE PERSON I LOST

1. I remember our relationship realistically with positive and negative memories. _____
2. I feel all right about not thinking about the loss for a time. I am not betraying the one I lost. _____
3. I no longer go on a search for my loved one. _____
4. I don't feel compelled to hang on to the pain. _____
5. The ways I keep my loved one alive are healthy and acceptable. _____
6. I can think about other things in life other than what I lost. _____
7. My life has meaning even though this person is gone. _____

CHANGES I HAVE MADE IN ADJUSTING TO MY NEW WORLD

1. I have integrated my loss into my world and I can relate to others in a healthy way. _____
2. I can accept the help and support of other people. _____
3. I can be open in my feelings in other relationships. _____
4. I feel it is all right for life to go on, even though my loved one is gone. _____
5. I have developed an interest in people and things outside myself and have no relationship to the person I lost. _____
6. I have put my loss in perspective. _____

SO NOW, DO YOU HAVE AN ANSWER TO THE QUESTION OF, "ARE YOU NORMAL"?

Because of who God is, we can be certain He has it all in control. If we understand He is the God of the Universe, we would know He can handle our little Universe of problems. Our problem is we want God to solve our problem now. We are used to instant satisfaction. We can have instant breakfast, lunch or dinner in less than 10 minutes. We can have instant emotions and mood change through medications in less than 5 minutes. We can have instant coffee in 2 minutes. We have instant communication by phone or pager in less than 1 minute. We can get instant money from a corner machine in less than 30 seconds. We have instant access to breaking world news in less than 1 second.

It's little wonder that we feel God is not going or doing for us fast enough. We want our fast paced problems fixed now and are not willing to wait on God's perfect timing. (Dobson, 1993, pp.40–59)

SEARCHING

They had been married for just twelve years. The marriage had been rocky at first, but the last few years were going along great. He was a youth minister at a local church. She worked part-time so she could spend most of her time with their young children. One day, their lives change forever. A terminal disease was discovered by the physician. Her short life ended just four months later.

One was a drunk driver. One was a faithful father of two little girls. A car went out of control. The drunk driver was sorry. The father was dead. The mother and the two little girls suffer. Why does this happen?

As one is in this time of searching, it is not unusual to ask the question "How long will I be like this?" The drive for this question comes from the understanding that things have a beginning and some sort of an ending. We like to have control. We like to know there is order to things. Unfortunately, when you are in the searching process it is not possible to know how long your pain, your grieving, your world, will be disorderly. Most people report the grieving, the searching, the questioning, all come in uncontrollable waves of emotions. The waves come in various intensity and frequency over several periods of time. But it does get better. Our defenses against our emotions get better. Our searching gets more refined. Our ability to cope with our new situation gets better. Holding on to the knowledge that we will make progress is important as you face the grief. There are no set time tables for searching. In the beginning the search seems to function as if we were on automatic pilot. We begin to just go through the motions of our life requirements. We can't seem to switch off our thoughts or switch on our thoughts when we have the need. Our feeling can be in control or out of control at a moment's notice.

The notion of control plays a huge role in the searching process. In most situations when someone experiences a trauma or tragic event they have little control over the outcome. Being out of control is a very uneasy process as it produces a vulnerability that affects your whole life experience. That's why the searching process is so important so that you can start to regain some control at a time when you feel as though you have very little control. The brain records all experiences and spins in its searching to find answers. Most tragedies have no logical explainable answers, so the searching continues.

DEAR GOD, WHY DID YOU PICK MY MOM?

"Mom is gone. Where are you, Mommy? Can you hear me? I was only twelve-years-old when Mom died. She was diagnosed with breast cancer at age 34. That was eight years ago. Of course, I didn't know what was wrong with Mom or how really sick she was. All I knew was that she would go to the doctor, come home, and have to go to sleep. My brother and I were not allowed to bother Mommy when she was sleeping. I was just a little kid who wanted Mommy to spend all her time with me and not sleep so much. I really didn't know I would have to watch my mother suffer and die before I was really old enough to understand.

I'm sixteen now, and I'm still trying to figure out why I had to lose my mom to God before she or I were ready. I guess I'm being selfish but I wanted Mom to watch me grow up. Isn't that the way life is supposed to be? She wasn't supposed to die and leave me alone. She was supposed to take care of me and my brother. Dear God, why did You pick my mother?

Don't get me wrong, I do have a wonderful dad who has done everything possible to make me happy over the past four years. He's Mom and Dad now. But something is missing. I keep thinking what it would be like if she were still alive. Is it wrong to wish she was still here? Am I feeling this way because there is so much I didn't get to tell her?

You know, my relationship with Mom wasn't the best. I wish I could say I was the perfect loving daughter. But that would be a lie. Perhaps because I knew she was dying I became bitter and pushed her away some. I gave her a hard time. I didn't mean to. I forgot she was sick because she was in remission for almost seven years. When she got really sick again the year before she died, I pretended she was fine. I never thought much about her dying. I thought I had control of my emotions. I thought if I didn't give in, she wouldn't die. It was my defense, and I fooled myself into believing it. Funny how, now that I am a little older, I can realize this.

That last year I watched Mom get weaker and weaker. She lost all her hair again, and she was so thin. I watched as she withered away and the cancer just ate her up alive. She couldn't get out of bed anymore and Grandma and Dad had to take care of her. All I could do was watch. I tried talking to her, but I felt she didn't understand me much. I gave her little reason to know me. Over the past few years, I just pushed her more and more away. I wonder now if I hurt her feelings. She never said anything to me about it, but I felt so distant. I loved her so much. Why couldn't I tell her.

I could see the pain in Grandma's eyes. She's trying to hide her feelings and act like everything is going to be just fine. But I knew everything wasn't okay and my life would never be the same again.

I felt like this wasn't real, like a dream, and that somehow it would all just disappear. You know, that's exactly what happened—Mom disappeared, just disappeared from my life. I can't complain to her anymore. I can't call her to help me when I need her. I can't tell her I love her. I can't tell her I'm sorry. She doesn't hear me. She doesn't answer me. Mom, where are you? Do you know what I'm doing or who I have become? Do you know how I feel? Can you see me? Were you there when I got my first A in school? I did it for you. You always told me I could do better. I feel so alone sometimes. You'd be proud of me now. I take care of myself. I work hard at school. I want to go to college. Are you listening, Mom? Do you hear me? Do you think I look like you, Mom? Am I pretty? I lost weight. I play sports and I love taking pictures, just like you did. I won third place in a photo contest. I took a picture of our shed. You remember, the shed with that old shovel just leaning against the rusty wall? Mom, I want to believe you hear me and are watching me grow up. I think I'll hold on to that thought. I love you.

I was thinking about why God picked my Mom, and I have to be honest, I don't understand God much yet, but I can only imagine that my Mom was someone really special to Him. Even though I wanted to keep her here with us, it wasn't my decision. She was only 42 and I guess it was her time to accept God's kiss of eternal life."

Author: Maria Rosa

We don't appreciate God more because of our losses. We don't look to him to provide instant answers so that we can have a light bulb moment in the midst of our personal trauma, so that we can say; "Now I know the reason for my problem. Wow. Now that I have discovered the answer I can go on with my life." It doesn't work like that. Your pain is real and your searching for answers is real. Somehow, and for some reason known only to God, you are to suffer this life situation. Don't misunderstand me. I am not suggesting that God sends the painful experience for our "growth" or to enhance our appreciation for the life we have been given. Nor am I implying the fullness of life comes only to those who have experienced triumph through personal tragedy. Rather, I am saying that God is present in all of life, including the traumas. His presence transforms even these agonizing experiences into opportunities for our search.

> If you suffer, thank God!!!—it is a sure sign that you are alive
>
> —Elbert Hubbard

You may believe that God is not doing anything to help in your recovery. It seems the more and the harder you search, the farther you are from the answers. We want recovery now. We want answers now. We do not want the pain associated with the search. God has a reason for everything He does and a specific time table not based on when we think we need answers. Give yourself permission to search, to not know the answer, to not know how to recover, to not know when you will recover, to be adrift in your grieving.

There is something so powerful in giving yourself permission to wait and to search until you can gain hope. God has a way of sending someone, some situation, some help, something, that only you can see that will give you hope.

SEARCHING

It's as ugly as it seems,
To wake up today and face broken dreams.
Dreams Hurt
It's a wicked delusion of reprieve,
To think that suffering will soon be relieved.
Suffering Hurts
The intense pain must and will be suffered.
Only by relationships can it be buffered.
Relationships Hurt
Survival means nothing left to lose,
It happens when reality has lost all clues.
Reality Hurts
Can one survive? Can one make the
transition?
How quick the people of steel become the
people of tin!
Change Hurts
Efforts and emotion reduced to one task,
Seeking wish-fulfillment behind the human
mask.
Life Hurts
The last of human freedom is the ability to
choose,
This precarious responsibility of self is the one
to lose.
Loss Hurts
"Oh God, these are all but concepts to You,
If You won't answer the searching questions,
then who?"

Answers Hurt
"Seek and find!" God loudly and silently cried.
"I experienced it all, when my Son hung there
and died"
God Hurts
Found the truth in utter painful desolation,
The meaning of life in the balance of salvation.
Jesus Heals

GOD GIVES MEANING IN SUFFERING

Regardless of the reason for suffering it will never leave the sufferer the same. It is doubtful that any other experience can so shape our life like that of grief. It has been said that if something doesn't kill you it makes you stronger. C.S. Lewis said, "God whispers to us in our pleasures, speaks in our conscience, but shouts in our pain; it is His megaphone to arouse a deaf world."

What does God teach us through our suffering? Some of the reasons may be:

1. Suffering forces us to walk by faith.
   We cannot know the mind of God. We cannot see the big picture. We only know a small slice of why, where, when, and how things happen. Sometimes by solving problems we are able to move forward in our faith journey. Sometimes it helps our obedience and patience as we share in suffering to learn to trust that He is in control.

> "The breaking of the alabaster box and the anointing of the Lord filled the house with the odor, with the sweetest odor. Everyone could smell it. Whenever you meet someone who has really suffered; been limited, gone through things for the Lord, willing to be imprisoned by the Lord, just being satisfied with Him and nothing else, immediately you smell the fragrance. There is a savor of the Lord. Something has been crushed, something has been broken, and there is a resulting odor of sweetness."
>
> —Watchman Nee

Since you left...
My life is so much lonelier without you.
I can't seem to trust anything or anyone.
They say they want to help, but don't know how.
No one has time to listen to my anxieties,
It scares them too much.
They think I don't know.
I see the anxiety it creates for them so I shut down.
They can't answer my questions.
Who is God?
How did this happen?
Where do I now fit in?
Will I ever be healthy?
Will I get answers?
Will I see you again?
What is fair?

Dwight Carlson, in his book *When Life Isn't Fair* makes the argument that even when God is in control it is not always clear to us. "The belief that God is in control of the universe leads some people to conclude He has planned every last detail and wants every event to come about exactly as it does. Such a God would delight in pushing misfortune buttons: this God says, 'Let's give Mary an *A* on her English test today. Let's give Joanne a dent in her fender. I'll clog up Pat's sink. Joe will get a heart attack, and I'll give Susan leukemia'" (Carlson, 1989, p.38).

> "It is not a question of God allowing or not allowing things to happen. It is a part of living. Some things we do to ourselves, other things we do to others. Our Father knows about every bird which falls to the ground, but He does not always prevent it from falling. What are we to learn from this? That our response to what happens is more important than what happens. Here is a mystery: one man's experience drives him to curse God, while another man's identical experience drives him to bless God. Your response to what happens is more important than what happens."
>
> —Chip Brogden

Genesis 22:1, the Bible tells us that God tested Abraham to take his son, Isaac, and offer him as a burnt offering. What a test of walking by faith!

On that stark mountain a few days later, the aged patriarch raised a sharpened knife—poised to plunge into the heart of the one he loved. (Think of it!) But God stepped in and stayed his hand.

You ask, "How could Abraham actually carry out such a plan in an obedient manner?" The answer is tucked away in Heb. 11:17–19, which says, "By faith Abraham, when he was tested, offered up Isaac; and he who had received the promises was offering up his only begotten son: it was he to whom it was said, 'In Isaac your descendants shall be called.' He considered that God is able to raise men even from the dead…"

Abraham was determined to shift the weight of his trust from himself to God, who "is able to raise men even from the dead." And this, the Bible calls *faith*.

> Pain plants the flag of reality
> In the fortress of a rebel heart.

Pain reduces us to a primary level, the level of dependence on our God. While we stretch out full length on Him, everything within us that is useless and abrasive is simply melted away. Those who were hard and harsh are humbled in Him. Those once proud and self-sufficient are drawn to their knees.

Suffering reveals our creature status. We are not all-wise or infinite in strength. But God is. And we need Him, *we were created to need Him*. Desperately. Sometimes it takes coming to the end of us to see that God knows. We need to take everything we were, everything we are, and everything we've ever hoped to be and simply place it all in the nail-scarred hands of our loving Lord.

It is interesting that children are the model for walking by faith. It seems Jesus is always referencing that we are to come to Him in "childlike" faith. We don't always get answers to our journey of suffering; because at times, God must treat us like children for a variety of reasons. (1) We can't see the big picture and how our pain and suffering fits into the larger scheme. In order for us to reach the destination God has to say no to some of our requests and demands. Can you imagine if God indulged and honored our requests, even if it wasn't good for us? God's overarching plan is for you to learn some things in life and to get to the destination that He has planned for your life. His itinerary includes some unpleasant stops along the journey that end up being good teaching spots for us. Most of our demands are unnecessary and in the grand scheme for us rather petty and self-serving. (2) God is on-time, every time, but not necessarily on our time schedule. God will bring people, circumstances, and situations in your life that makes no sense at the time. It is hard for us to imagine that He has the timing to know when to intervene, but He does. (3) God understands the beginning from the end, and we only see the present. For some of you, the journey has been long and stormy and the difficulties along the way have been incredible. You have had to give up lifelong partners, have bodies that wore out before your mind did, gave up children before you were ready, had spouses that didn't want to walk by faith and they walked out on you. Walking by faith is a hard concept, one that a person doesn't ask for, they only experience.

2. Suffering helps us to focus on what is really important.

   When someone close to you dies, it's really amazing how unimportant other things become. We can then develop a proper evaluation of what's important. We will note how material things are only temporary and how relationships are permanent. We can evaluate our career, work habits, health, values, goals, and what place God has in our life. Its true circumstances don't make or break us; it only reveals what our base is built upon.

> "Character cannot be developed in ease and quiet. Only through experience of trial and suffering can the soul be strengthened, ambition inspired, and success achieved."
>
> —Helen Keller

Is This My Trial?
The pain has been so awful,
I don't know if the journey is worth it.
I've learned too many things,
And now I can't stand the suffering.
Where has my strength gone?
What am I supposed to learn?
Did I do something so wrong?
Do I need to be punished?

Tell me who I have offended, and I will
confess.
I will give myself to them.
If only the pain will stop.
I have been robbed of my very life.
I learned I can survive.

> My barn having burned to the ground, I can now see the moon
>
> —Masahide

Once upon a time, a king decided that if he could ask the right questions and get just the right answers, then he would always know what to do in any situation. He called his wise counselors together and after several days of discussion, the counselors proposed that three questions in any situation will guide you in the path of life: What is life all about? How do I fit? Who am I?

The king was impressed and asked the wise counselors to then answer the questions. He received various answers but none satisfied him. One of the wise counselors consulted with the king and suggested the only way to truly answer the questions is to go on a journey of discovery and to find out for himself. The king traveled in the valley, along rivers, through storms, in the hot day and the cold nights, finally coming to a high mountain. The king asked everyone he encountered to give him an answer to the three questions. It seems no one had an answer that satisfied the king. On top of the mountain, he met a man. The king asked him the three questions. The man, digging in his garden, listened to the king talk about his journey to find the answers to the three questions. The king explained that he had talked to a lot of people, had endured a long and painful journey, and still didn't know the answer to the three questions. The man said nothing and returned to digging in his garden. The king, instead of being insulted as he would have been before the journey, said "Give me the shovel while you think on my questions, and I will dig while you rest." The man rested, still said nothing, and the king dug in the garden. After several hours, the king was very tired. He put down the shovel and said, "If you can't answer my questions, that's all right. Just tell me, and I'll take my leave." The man laughed and said, "Your questions are already answered. Tell me what you learned on your journey." The king thought and thought and finally said, "What I have learned is that (1) some questions will have no suitable answer, (2) I learned about myself on the journey, (3) if I had not made the journey, I would have not struggled with the questions.

My Year Left Me
Another year has come and gone.
My year no longer controls me.
I am no longer afraid.
To live or question is the same for me.
He is with me on this journey.
I call out in the world.
They respond but I can't see the light.
I struggle with the meaning of what I am
doing.

No answers are ever satisfied.
Questions never produced happiness.
Answers didn't provide.
He provides.

3. Suffering will bring to focus our need for God. The shortest road to God is when we have personal grief. In the Apostle Paul's suffering, he learned the value of giving thanks in everything. We don't know if today will bring sorrow or pleasure, but we know God does, and sometimes it has to be enough.

> "You may never know that Jesus is all you need, until Jesus is all you have"
>
> —Corrie Ten Boom

Because of Paul's encounter with affliction, many were led to focus on the Lord Jesus Christ and give thanks. One man offered praise in his moment of sorrow, and God so multiplied his song it became a great chorus, echoing in antiphonal voice from heart after heart.

God is interested in using us as *living* object lessons to others. That is precisely why He urges us to present ourselves as *living* sacrifices. What might happen in your life if you stopped fighting God and started to praise Him for your pain? We all fear pain; yet from the day of our birth we experience pain. Pain serves as a warning system that something is wrong, that something needs to be changed, that we need to do something different. Sometimes our only comfort is to know that God, in the form of Jesus, experienced all the same pain that we could ever experience. When we cry out to God, we can have the faith to know that He has had the experience. He hears. He understands. He cares. He has been there.

Try telling Him that you want to be His living object lesson of patience and stability to others. Tell Him how grateful you are for the crushing blows He has chosen to bring into your life.

In your own way and in your own words, express how very thankful you are that He has selected you from the ranks of millions to share in "the fellowship of His sufferings," and like Christ, to "learn obedience for the things which you suffer." You will be a rare, refined believer if you respond to suffering in this manner, child of God.

> "Far too often, however, we resent and resist any interference on God's part that might deprive us of our deepest desires. We are bitter and hostile toward God and mourn over our "victimization" at His hands. We constantly remind Him how much we are doing for Him despite His lack of reciprocity."
>
> —Jim Owen

Job responded in a similar manner when he said, "Why should I take my flesh in my own teeth, and put my life in my hands? Though He slay me, I will hope in Him" (Job 13:14–15).

If Job could lift his face and say that to God, so can you. "Lord, even though this is the most difficult experience of my life, my hope is in You. Thank You for this canyon of pain. I'm leaning on You as I go through it."

A whole new dimension is opened up to the one who learns to give God thanks for his plan...pain notwithstanding. When you are able to be comforted by the very God who created the world, it brings your spiritual life into a new dimension. Before your trauma you could easily keep God at a safe distance. Sure, He was important, but so was your job, your educational achievements, your career, your money, your family, your friends, your place in the company ladder. Then came the trauma that ripped it away. Depression fell like a foggy night. Turn to your job to help? Your career helped you find peace? Family and friends deserted you? Money ran out? Your college degree gave you security? The trauma wasn't impressed with your status in life. Suddenly you were left with one option, the One who never fails, who always loves, who always cares for you. It's sad that we have to experience trauma, suffering, and grief before we can experience Him.

> "Blessings alone do not open our eyes. Indeed, blessings by themselves tend to close our eyes. We do not come to know Him in the blessing, but in the breaking."
>
> —Chip Brogden

How Do I Explain This?
Trauma found me.
Who really knows how it feels?
Who rescues me from me?
Words and feelings to our own song.
Memories flood the tears in our eyes.
And how the heart aches to no end.
Trauma found me.
My nights are filled with restless sleep.
My days are mild illusions of my former self.
I cry out to God.
No answer, because trauma found me.
Alone I fight the pain, the loss, the sorrow.
I don't want to see tomorrow.
I try to understand words that feel so cold
Trauma found me.
Others experience the same.
I don't see how this helps me become human.
Trauma found me.

4. Suffering gives us an experience we can relate to others.

   Who better understands what it's like to have a child die? To sit with a dying relative who has a terminal disease? The person who has been there is probably among the most qualified. You are the first choice counselor God can call on to help others.

> "It is highly significant, and indeed almost a rule, that moral courage has its source in identification through one's own sensitivity with the suffering of one's fellow human beings."
>
> —Rollo May

> "These things I have spoken to you that you may have peace. In the world, you will have many problems, but take courage, because I have overcome the world."
>
> —Jesus Christ

God knows how we suffer, and He is big enough to allow us to express our suffering. In working with people who are in the midst of their suffering, we have found the following to be helpful exercises.

ANGER EXPRESSION

Turn your anger into a verbal argument with God. "God I am so angry with this situation! I can't stand this emotional pain! I find it really hard that You are allowing this to happen to me! It's not fair! I hurt badly! I am angry with You! Make my pain go away! I trusted You! How much do You expect me to endure? I am past my limit!"

Physical exercise while being verbal is recommended. Try moving around to move the stuck energy in your body. Those pent up emotions need to work itself outside of your body. Do something physical as long as it is not self-destructive.

THANKFUL JOURNAL

Purchase a blank journal and begin writing all the things you can remember about your past life before the trauma. Make it a positive experience. Enlist the support of others to help you remember. Use photos, e-mails, and greeting cards to invoke positive memories. Try to list three to five things a day in your journal of past people, places, or things for which you are thankful. You will not "feel like it" but use your thinking skills to help you. No matter how painful it is, expressing gratitude for your past positive experiences can help you remember you have a life to live in the future.

BALANCED LIFESTYLE

Write at the top of your journal the word "person." This is to remind you that you have not given up your personhood because of this tragedy. The word "person" will form the basis for starting a suffering recovery program.

P will stand for physical. You need to develop a small physical goal for the day. It can be as simple as getting out of bed and taking a shower/bath. You need to get moving and not become stagnant in your suffering. The next day develop a little larger physical goal. Get out of bed, take a shower/bath and walk outside for ten minutes. Continue to build success on your physical goals by adding a little more each day. Don't worry about "not feeling like it," just do what you know will move you forward.

PHYSICAL HEALTH QUIZ:

1. Describe how you will balance your nutrition this week? Are you taking vitamins? Are you eating regular meals? Are you overweight or underweight?
   Give yourself a grade: A, B, C, D, F to the following:
   What you put in your body (eating and drinking) ________________
   What you have done to your body (pace, workload, pressure) ________________
   What you have done for your body (exercise) ________________
   How you have treated your body (rest, sleep, relaxation) ________________
2. What will you do to improve your sleep? Do you have trouble falling asleep or staying asleep? Do you feel suddenly awake when you get into bed?

E will stand for emotional. Developing an emotional goal each day is essential for your recovery. Suffering will sap all of your emotional strength and insight if you don't move forward. Emotional goals need to center around the question, "What will bring me pleasure?" You can filter the answer through these thoughts:

What and who matter the most to me?

What helps my spiritual support system?
How might I be of value to others?
What have I done in the past that brought me pleasure?
What possessions do I still have that bring me comfort?
What can I do to make life worthwhile?
How do I want people who love me to remember me?

EMOTIONAL HEALTH QUIZ:

1. What negative feelings will you most likely experience this week? List the feelings with possible positive ways to manage them.
2. What small but reasonable emotional change can you make this week?
3. Life has not turned out like any of us expected. What is your current expectation of what life will be like one year from now?
4. If a miracle occurs and you could understand the purpose for your life, what would it be?
5. What do you need to accomplish with your life in the next thirty days?

R stands for relationships. When you strip life down to its basic form, all we have left is relationships. Who do you need to be grateful for that is still in your life? Who could be encouraged by your moving forward in the suffering? What one thing could you do today for someone else? Who has been ministering to you in your suffering?

RELATIONAL QUIZ:

1. If conflict arises this week with another person, the other person is likely to be whom?
2. What can you do to manage this conflict?
3. List one small but reasonable positive action you will do this week to benefit someone else.
4. Name several people who you feel close to.
5. What support group can you explore to get back in touch with people?

S stands for spiritual. Now is a great time to relook at your spiritual life. We always suggest a good spiritual inventory at this time in your suffering stage.

SPIRITUAL QUIZ:

1. Have you ever had religious or spiritual beliefs or practices? What was helpful or harmful?
2. Who or what has been an influence on your religious or spiritual beliefs?
3. What has been your most profound spiritual experience?
4. Write down your religious or spiritual beliefs about the following: humans, God, relationships, marriage.
5. What do you think is your purpose for being alive?

6. To you, who is Jesus Christ; for example, a good man, a world leader, a crazy man, or God/man in the flesh?
7. Define heaven and hell.
8. When you die, what happens to you?
9. What do you do or where do you go to "recharge or refocus" when you get a chance?
10. How do you connect with other people?
11. Where do you contribute or be of service to others or to the world?
12. If you could write a prayer right now, what would it be?
13. What kind of spiritual activities would you like to do in the future?
14. Is there any area of your spiritual life you would like to develop more?
15. Who do you know has an active spiritual life that could be a role model for you?

The last two letters in P-E-R-S-ON means to get on with it. The grieving process only lessons when you take action to move forward. Nothing changes unless you change it. You may not be able to change the circumstances of the tragedy, but you can help yourself do self-care activities and not self-destructive activities. Suffering will affect every area of your being, from physical, emotional, relational, and spiritual. Recovery also needs to occur in all areas. There are important things to remember as you are developing your balance in the midst of suffering.

1. It is done in your time frame. Not anyone else's time frame. There are no good "models" for how long suffering takes. Don't allow suffering to be too short or too long. As long as you are doing self-care and not self-destructive behaviors, then the pace is correct. You will have to deal with several "first time events" in your suffering. Here's some practical advice of facing them.

    a. The first holiday after the tragedy. Holidays are usually an exciting time for family and friends; a time of getting together, of laughter, and intimacy. These were once times of great joy for you, but now may fill you with heartache, anxiety, depression, and dread. You might have all kinds of mixed emotions, and there will be different opinions among your loved ones about how to celebrate or acknowledge these times. Like all first events, it's important to do something to acknowledge the holiday. You may choose to do what you have always done for these events. You may choose to do something different, but do something. The key is to acknowledge the holiday and to do something. Do not wait for your feelings to be your guide, use your thinking skills to drive this process. Some people feel they are getting worse right before and during the holidays. It is hard to go about your daily business of life and not see the holiday being promoted in western culture. The best thing you can do is to talk to friends and family about what your expectations for the holiday entail. The worst thing you can do is to ignore the holiday or not speak to your loved ones about the holiday. Open a line of communication with them to express your wishes, so they are not kept guessing about what you want to do. Any festive holiday requires lots of energy. You may not have the energy to give to shopping, cooking, presents, sending, and receiving cards. Most people find these times of the year tiring and stressful, too. So, with the energy it takes to deal with a tragedy, preparing for a holiday may be an unrealistic expectation you are placing on yourself. Be realistic about what you can do. If you feel like it's all overwhelming, then cut back on your normal routines and let this first holiday be calm.

b. The first anniversary of the tragedy. The reality of life is that it goes forth. Before you know it, one year will have passed after the tragedy. Some people find they begin to experience unexpected anxiety or depression weeks before the first anniversary. It is not uncommon to experience a similar reaction to the one you experienced a year ago. You may have trouble sleeping again, trouble concentrating again, trouble eating again, troubling dreams again, emotional outbursts again. You may feel disappointed with yourself, because you have made so much progress. If you expect the first anniversary to be difficult, you'll be less likely to be critical of yourself and just feel the emotions. You have learned by now this first will pass at some point.

c. Unexpected first time events. There will be many firsts that you will not see coming until they overwhelm you. You feel as though you have been hit out of the blue and rocked your world almost as powerful as the actual tragedy. This trigger event will not be surface noticeable and may be triggered by a smell, a song, a color, a cologne/perfume, seeing someone unexpectedly, or a past lost memory. It is impossible to predict what they might be or when it might happen. The best way to deal with the event is to pause. Pause where you are and give yourself time to think. Challenge any irrational thoughts, and remind yourself you are in the present and you are safe and you will overcome this sudden feeling.

Developing plans, no matter how simple they are, will make it easier to face events when you are grieving. The first event to concern you may be a date that signified a happy occasion, such as a birthday or anniversary. Or it may mark a difficult time such as the date when you received the news of the diagnosis or when your loved one died. Whenever a significant date approaches, think about the following questions as you make your plans. What would you like to do to acknowledge the date? Is there someone you would like to be with on that date? Is there anything specific you want to do? What arrangements do you need to make ahead of time? How can you carve out time to just be with your grief? (Morris, 2008, p.185)

2. If you need time alone or with others then ask for it. Others can't read your mind. They do not know exactly what you need. Sometimes it will be that you need some time alone to cry, to be angry, to talk to God, to talk ugly to God. Other times, you just can't be alone. Ask someone to stay with you during these times. Friends and family are waiting on you to share what you need.
3. Give yourself permission. You need to be who God made you to be. If you need to laugh inappropriately, then do it. If you need to cry inappropriately, then do it. If you need to "be crazy" for a period of time, find a safe place and let yourself be crazy. If you need to be afraid, then be fearful for a time. There is no destination when you arrive, only the journey of getting there. Don't expect too much of yourself in the suffering stage.
4. Commit to the future. You will live. You will need to plan for it. Don't be talked into spending money you don't have for something you can't afford. Commitment to the future allows you to believe you can face all the fears, uncertainty, hurts, frustrations, and pain of today. You will

have to experience the pain of the present, but you will need to live in the future.

One of the ways we can commit to the future is to identify why we want to live. Use the following assessment to gain insight into your reasons.

REASONS FOR LIVING ASSESSMENT:

I have a responsibility and commitment to my family.
I believe I can learn to adjust to, or cope with, my problems.
I believe I have control over my life and destiny.
I believe only God has the right to end a life.
I want to watch my children as they grow.
Life is all we have and is better than nothing.
I have future plans I am looking forward to carrying out.
No matter how bad I feel, I know that it will not last.
I love and enjoy my family too much and could not leave them.
I am afraid that my method of killing myself would fail.
I want to experience all that life has to offer, and there are many experiences I have not had yet that I want to have.
It would not be fair to leave the children for others to take care of.
I have a love of life.

I am too stable to kill myself.
My religious beliefs forbid it.
The effect on my children could be harmful.
It would hurt my family too much and I would not want them to suffer.
I am concerned about what others would think of me.
I consider it morally wrong.
I still have many things left to do.
I have the courage to face life.
I believe killing myself would not really accomplish or solve anything.
Others would think I am weak and selfish.
I would not want people to think I did not have control over my life.
I would not want my family to feel guilty afterward.

> "The doorbell rang at around eight-thirty. I wasn't expecting anyone, so a strange feeling came over my heart. I peeked out the keyhole, and saw my brother and sister-in-law. I let them in the house. There was deep silence, and I knew from my brother's eyes what had happened. He didn't have to speak. He took me in his arms, and my world changed forever. My eyes moved to a picture of my son on the mantel and I knew he was gone. My world turned to darkness, and I would never live the same way again.
>
> Singer Judy Collins on learning of the death of her son"

REDEFINING LIFE

By now you've come to the realization life will never be the same. To be healthy, you must choose to start the process of re-evaluation of life with your focus on change. This is what you will come to understand about your grieving process:

> Your grief will cause major changes to every area of your life.
> Your grief will take a lot longer to manage than you can even imagine.
> You will never recover but you will be in a recovering mode from your loss.
> Your grieving process will include your past, present, and perception of the future.
> Your grieving process will come sometimes suddenly and without warning.
> You will not go crazy from your grieving process.
> Your grief may bring up old issues that you have carried as baggage into your present life.

> You will feel things, say things, and do things that you would not have done without the traumatic experience.
> You will redefine your life if you choose to do the work it will require.

When we experience the death of a loved one, trauma, tragedy, or any of life's huge downs, we lose a piece of ourselves. The closer our relationship to the person, the more of our self we have to redefine. Much of our human identity comes from other humans. Defining our self as a spouse/partner, husband/wife, sister/brother can bring satisfaction to life; but when faced with loss, it also means we must redefine the resulting emptiness. Emptiness is a temporary feeling. You won't and can't know where it will lead your life. Redefining means that you don't need to know all the answers now. It takes time. It means to search, to look, to ask questions, to seek honesty, to be willing to be different, to be open to new experiences, courage to step outside your comfort zone. For some, this process takes months; for some, it takes a lifetime, but piece by piece you can redefine your life. Life will never be the same. It will be your new life and it will be different.

What Have I Become?
Lost.
Empty.
I am trying to redefine my life.
I can't and won't let me in.
No person.
Lost identity.
I am trying to redefine my life.

I can't and won't let me in.
Spouse?
Significant other?
I am trying to redefine my life.
I can't and won't let me in.
Career?
Roles in life.
I am trying to redefine my life.
I can't and won't let me in.
Helpless, hopeless, worthless.

Grief is not an ending or a walking away from what we have lost. Forgetting the person or the dream that died is not the same as recovery from loss. Recovery from loss allows us to reshape our relationship with the person or the dream we have lost and to find ways to grow in our new circumstances.

Mary Beth Chapman details the highs and lows of her life in her memoir, *Choosing to SEE: A Journey of Struggle and Hope.* Chapman and her husband, Grammy Award-winning musician, Steven Curtis Chapman, suffered a terrible tragedy in 2008 when their five-year-old daughter died after accidentally being hit by an SUV that was being driven by their son. In her book, Mary Beth Chapman shares what it's like to be the wife of a star musician and opens up about the pain of her daughter's death. She details the pain, the fears, and the ongoing struggle with trying to understand all the questions of this tragedy. She ends up telling us that in the midst of it all, that God has been with them to provide comfort in the questions of the tragedy. She freely shares that the questions outweigh the answers of her life. "When people ask how we are doing, the first thing I always say is, 'I want Maria back. I want my son Will Franklin not to have this as a chapter in his story. I want my children to be healthy, my family secure. I don't really care whose life has been touched or changed because of our loss!'" That is the heart of a mother who lost a daughter and is determined not to lose another child. "I believe God can handle my heart, my questions, and my anger. It's okay to want Maria back. It's okay to be angry. The question is what do I do with it all? What do I do with God? In the midst of such heartbreak, do I really believe that all things work together for good for those who love him and are called according to his purpose?"

One of the most demanding challenges of grief involves reinvesting in life. New relationships, new dreams are offered to us. New joy is possible. That which is new, however, may feel very uncomfortable. We may feel it is somehow wrong to experience the joys of life again. We will be acutely aware that any time we open ourselves to new love or to new hope that we also open ourselves to the possibility of new loss.

We know that we are reinvesting in life when we are active in the recovery process. Norman Wright writes in his book, *Crisis and Trauma Counseling,* "Is Recovery ever complete? Not really. The issues can be reawakened from time to time. But we gradually experience:

- Fears will diminish

  How can a person tell if they are progressing? First of all, they can expect to see a reduction in the frequency of symptoms. In addition, the intensity of fear they struggle with over the presence of these symptoms will diminish. One of the fears that is so disheartening is the fear of going crazy or insane. This fear will also diminish.

> "No one told me that grief felt so like fear."
>
> —C.S. Lewis

Anger will subside

Anger and grief, which exist hand in hand, will lessen. What remains can be directed into positive actions. However, there will be times the only way to rid the anger is to face the fact they can't change the past or prevent the future. They can learn to give up a portion of anger or resentment day by day. Anger normally has an identifiable cause, something we can attach our emotion to, an event, a trauma, a tragedy. The idea behind challenging your irrational thoughts is to move toward a shift in your thinking. Let your thought control your emotions. The emotions will take up your energy to live. It will prevent you from experiencing the healing process of redefining your life. Challenging your irrational thoughts is not a cure all for the real experience. What you are attempting to do is to ensure your thinking is helpful and accurate about the events surrounding your life. Anger's emotions will eat you up and has the effect of getting you stuck in your emotions. Anger is sometimes a means of experiencing control in an out of control situation. It is a healthy defense mechanism if used correctly and a barrier to recovery if allowed to run free. This emotional response is an attempt to answer the questions that have been created by your loss. We realize that we are helpless to change the event, and it produces this intense emotional response. If we are careful this process can be healthy and therapeutic.

> "Grief is not a disorder, a disease or a sign of weakness. It is an emotional, physical and spiritual necessity, the price you pay for love. The only cure for grief is to grieve."
>
> —Earl Grollman

Rigidity will decrease

As you move through the journey of recovery, the rigidity that helps you cope will diminish. One will gradually discover the value of flexibility and spontaneity to a comfortable degree, which is based upon ones unique personality type.

> "When your fear touches someone's pain, it becomes pity. When your love touches someone's pain, it becomes compassion."
>
> —Stephen Levine

- Appreciation will abound

  One of the delights of recovery is developing a new appreciation of life. You begin to see what you didn't see before, to hear what you couldn't hear before, and taste what was tasteless before. Some people rediscover their sense of humor and all its healing properties.

  You will discover a new and deeper sense of empathy for the wounded around you.

> Grief is a normal and natural response to loss. It is originally an unlearned feeling process. Keeping grief inside increases your pain.
>
> —Ann Grant

- Improvements will be noted

  A common struggle in the recovery process is the ability to see and measure one's progress. For years, I've had people keep a daily or weekly journal in which they explicitly write what they are experiencing or feeling. These records, over time, make people more aware of their progress in a tangible way" (Wright, 2003, pp.232–234).

> "There is something you must always remember. You are braver than you believe, stronger than you seem, and smarter than you think."
>
> —Winnie the Pooh

- Decisions will become easier

Before you get to the other side of grief, you actually need to decide that this is what you want to do. It might seem like a "choice-less-choice," but it's important to have a conversation with yourself about why it's necessary to move forward and what it means to you. You can find yourself at a crossroads when you know deep down you need to make a decision, but you're not quite sure how to go about doing it. It is critical to understand that moving forward does not require you to forget your past life before the tragedy. Rather, it means finding ways to live your life again with a sense of purpose. Dr. Jerry Duncan is a private practice psychologist and a college professor. He takes his clients and students through a decision-making grid that he states "will help them not make an impulsive decision." Dr. Duncan states that step one is to ask yourself the question, "What is the problem or decision that you feel internal pressure to answer?" He says that we need a clarification of knowing if the pressure is an internal one or an external one. Also, it helps us clarify the symptoms from the problem. Step two, "How many solutions can you develop to manage the problem/decision?" He feels that by listing solutions, we begin to think rather than feel. This helps us move from irrational feelings to rational thinking. Step three, "What are the positives and negatives of each possible solution." We need to explore the old and new solutions to possibly break out of our old, bad patterns of thinking and behaving. The old ways of thinking become barriers to our changing. Step four, "What are the consequences of the new possible solutions." This defining possibly will help us create new patterns by becoming aware that we can make new choices. Step five, "What action will you take as a result of your decision?" If we are all attitude and no action, then nothing changes. We need to take small, but reasonable changes and not be afraid to fail.

> "We can endure much more than we think we can; all human experience testifies to that. All we need to do is learn not to be afraid of pain. Grit your teeth and let it hurt. Don't deny it, don't be overwhelmed by it. It will not last forever. One day, the pain will be gone and you will still be there."
>
> —Harold Kushner When All You've Ever Wanted Isn't Enough

In Dr. H. Bruch's book, *Learning Psychotherapy,* she states that basically all patients come to psychiatrists with "one common problem: the sense of helplessness, the fear and inner conviction of being unable to 'cope' and to change things." The entirety of our lives we are constantly making choices. We are making decisions as we face our problems. Jesus states that we will always have problems but will be able to work through problems by relying on his power. "These things I have spoken to you that in Me you may have peace. In the world you will have many problems, but I have overcome the world" (John 16:33).

> "The will of God is never exactly what you expect it to be. It may seem to be much worse, but in the end it's going to be a lot better and a lot bigger."
>
> —Elisabeth Elliott

One of my personal mentors, Charlie Baker, who coauthored *The Road To Recovery,* insists on signing his books "Thanks for being." I asked Charlie, "Thanks for being what?"

He explains to me that he wants people to know they are important; they are important to God, they are important to themselves, they are important to others. Charlie helps people see the need to change their self-concept as they begin to think differently about their life situations. Charlie is able to interact with people in a way that proves he cares for them, they can trust him, and he has their best "being" at heart. Charlie Baker is a light in the human race, a role model for us what it means to be a Christ-like representative to others around us. I have been convinced over and over that God brings certain people in Charlie's everyday life to be ministered to in such a way because of his "being" available.

WHO AM I?

However, when you experience a traumatic event, it feels so alone. It seems you are the only person in the world who has experienced such an event.

It appears like no one else in the world can understand the storm of life that you are experiencing. You begin to question, that if you are a child of God, then where is God? Doesn't He care that I am in a storm? Who am I to God? Max Lucado in his book, *In the Eye of the Storm*, presents a word picture of what it is like to be a disciple in the storm.

"Immediately Jesus made the disciples get into the boat and go on ahead of Him to the other side, while He dismissed the crowd. After He had dismissed them, He went up on a mountainside by Himself to pray. When evening came, He was there alone, but the boat was already a considerable distance from land, buffeted by the waves because the wind was against it." Matthew 14:22-24

"Matthew is specific about the order of events. Jesus sent the disciples to the boat. Then he dismissed the crowd and ascended a mountainside. It was evening, probably around 6:00 p.m. The storm struck immediately. The sun had scarcely set before the typhoon-like winds began to roar.

Note that Jesus sent the disciples out into the storm alone. Even as he ascended the mountainside, he could feel and hear the gale's force. Jesus was not ignorant of the storm. He was aware that a torrent was coming that would carpet bomb the sea's surface. But He didn't turn around. The disciples were left to face the storm... alone.

The greatest storm that night was not in the sky; it was in the disciples' hearts. The greatest fear was not from seeing the storm-driven waves; it came from seeing the back of their leader as He left them to face the night with only questions as companions.

It was this fury that the disciples were facing that night. Imagine the incredible strain of bouncing from wave to wave in a tiny fishing vessel. One hour would weary you. Two hours would exhaust you. Surely Jesus will help us, they thought. They'd seen Him still storms like this before. On this same sea, they had awakened Him during a storm, and He had commanded the skies to be silent. They'd seen Him quiet the wind and sooth the waves.

Surely he will come off the mountain. But He doesn't. Their arms begin to ache from rowing. Still no sign of Jesus. Three hours. Four hours. The winds rage. The boat bounces. Still no Jesus. Midnight comes. Their eyes search for God—in vain.

By now the disciples have been on the sea for as long as six hours. All this time, they have fought the storm and sought the Master. And, so far, the storm is winning. And the Master is nowhere to be found. "Where is He?" cried one. "Has He forgotten us?" yelled another. "He feeds thousands of strangers and yet leaves us to die?" muttered a third.

The Gospel of Mark adds compelling insight into the disciples' attitude. "They had not understood about the loaves; their hearts were hardened" (Mark 6:52).

What does Mark mean? Simply this, the disciples were mad. They begin the evening in a huff. Their hearts were hardened toward Jesus, because He fed the multitude. Their preference, remember, had been to "send the crowds away." Matthew 14:15. And Jesus told them to feed the people. But they wouldn't try. They said it couldn't be done. They told Jesus to let the people take care of themselves.

Also keep in mind that the disciples had just spent some time on center stage. They had tasted stardom. They were celebrities. They had rallied crowds. They had recruited an army. They were, no doubt, pretty proud of themselves. With chests a bit puffy and heads a bit swollen, they had told Jesus, "Just send them away." Jesus didn't. Instead, He chose to bypass the reluctant disciples and use the faith of an anonymous boy. What the disciples said could not be done, was done—in spite of them, not through them. They pouted. They sulked. Rather than being amazed at the miracle, they became mad at the Master. After all, they had felt foolish passing out the very bread they said could not be made. Add to that, Jesus' command to go to the boat when they wanted to go to battle, and it's easier to understand why these guys are burning!

"Now what is Jesus up to, leaving us out on the sea on a night like this?"

Peter, Andrew, James, and John have seen storms like this. They are fisherman; the sea is their life. They know the havoc the gale-force winds can wreak. They've seen the splintered hulls float to shore. They've attended the funerals. They know, better than anyone, that this night could be their last. “Why doesn’t He come?” they sputter.

Jesus came. He finally came. But between verses 24—being buffeted by waves—and verse 25—when Jesus appeared—a thousand questions are asked.

Questions you have probably asked too. Perhaps you know the angst of being suspended between verses 24 and 25. Maybe you’re riding a storm, searching the coastline for a light—a glimmer of hope. You know that Jesus knows what you are going through. You know that He is aware of your storm. But as hard you look to find Him, you can’t see Him. Maybe your heart, like the disciples’ hearts, has been hardened by unmet expectations. Your pleadings for help are salted with angry questions” (Lucado, 1991, pp.108–111.).

Alone Time!
I have lost my identity?
Alone time!
I do not know who I am?
Alone Time!
The process of re-establishment of me is too scary?
Alone Time!
I don’t know how to start?
Alone Time!
Where do I turn?
Alone Time!
Who will help me?
Alone Time!

We can also take action to increase our self-worth. The following are practical ideas to take action that will increase our sense of worth.

1. Share your memories with friends and family and get them to share theirs too. You may learn things that you didn't know about your loved one.

Action taken on what date:
How I felt doing it:
How I feel now:
How this action has helped me redefine life:

2. Leave flowers at your church or another special spot such as the beach, in the mountains, forest, at a river, or any peaceful spot.

Action taken on what date:
How I felt doing it:
How I feel now:
How this action has helped me redefine life:

3. Create a memory box containing special items that belonged to you and your loved one. Place little notes in it with special memories written on them.

Action taken on what date:
How I felt doing it:
How I feel now:
How this action has helped me redefine life:

4. Put notes into a box with a lock on it. Place messages into this box and write things down, which you wish you had said to your loved one before they passed away.

Action taken on what date:
How I felt doing it:
How I feel now:
How this action has helped me redefine life:

5. Make a collage of all your favorite photographs of your loved one and put it up on the wall where you can look at it anytime you like.

Action taken on what date:
How I felt doing it:
How I feel now:
How this action has helped me redefine life:

6. Honor your loved one's favorite tradition.

Action taken on what date:
How I felt doing it:
How I feel now:

How this action has helped me redefine life:

7. Create a new tradition in remembrance of your loved one. For example, you could light a candle and listen to your loved one's favorite music on the fifteenth day of every month.

Action taken on what date:
How I felt doing it:
How I feel now:
How this action has helped me redefine life:

8. Hang a stocking at Christmas containing lots of loving memories of your loved one.

Action taken on what date:
How I felt doing it:
How I feel now:
How this action has helped me redefine life:

9. Gather your friends and family together in celebration of your loved one. Perhaps throw a remembrance party on the anniversary of their death.

Action taken on what date:
How I felt doing it:
How I feel now:
How this action has helped me redefine life:

10. Light a candle in your loved one's memory.

Action taken on what date:
How I felt doing it:
How I feel now:
How this action has helped me redefine life:

11. Make a memory book of photos and memoirs of your loved one.

Action taken on what date:
How I felt doing it:
How I feel now:
How this action has helped me redefine life:

12. Donate money to a charity, or donate your time to help those less fortunate than you.

Action taken on what date:
How I felt doing it:
How I feel now:
How this action has helped me redefine life:

13. Wear a photo pin of your loved one or put their picture into a locket to treasure always.

Action taken on what date:
How I felt doing it:
How I feel now:
How this action has helped me redefine life:

14 Start a memorial trust or scholarship fund for your loved one.

Action taken on what date:
How I felt doing it:
How I feel now:
How this action has helped me redefine life:

15. Write a poem or a story about your loved one.

Action taken on what date:
How I felt doing it:
How I feel now:
How this action has helped me redefine life:

16. Visit a place that you used to like going to together. Remember the good times you had there.

Action taken on what date:
How I felt doing it:
How I feel now:
How this action has helped me redefine life:

17. Hang a special trinket or ornament from the Christmas tree.

Action taken on what date:
How I felt doing it:
How I feel now:
How this action has helped me redefine life:

18. Plant a tree in memorial of your loved one. Place a plaque next to the tree with a message on it.

Action taken on what date:
How I felt doing it:
How I feel now:
How this action has helped me redefine life:

19. Listen to your loved one's favorite music.

Action taken on what date:
How I felt doing it:
How I feel now:
How this action has helped me redefine life:

20. Cook the favorite meal of your love one and think of them while you are eating it.

Action taken on what date:
How I felt doing it:
How I feel now:
How this action has helped me redefine life:

21. Make a memorial quilt in your loved one's memory. You could even make it out of their old clothes.

Action taken on what date:
How I felt doing it:
How I feel now:
How this action has helped me redefine life:

22. Release balloons with friends and family in memory of your loved one. Perhaps attach little notes onto the balloons with messages on them.

Action taken on what date:
How I felt doing it:
How I feel now:
How this action has helped me redefine life:

23. Visit your loved one's resting place often and take flowers to leave at their grave.

Action taken on what date:
How I felt doing it:
How I feel now:
How this action has helped me redefine life:

24. Plant a memory garden for your loved one, plant their favorite flowers and trees and every time you are tending to it you will remember your loved one.

Action taken on what date:
How I felt doing it:
How I feel now:
How this action has helped me redefine life:

25. Write a letter to your lost loved one, tell them everything you are missing about them and everything that you learned from them.

Action taken on what date:
How I felt doing it:
How I feel now:
How this action has helped me redefine life:

26. If you are attending an event, such as a wedding or birthday, do something to remember your loved one at that special time, to show how much you wish they could be there with you.

Action taken on what date:
How I felt doing it:
How I feel now:
How this action has helped me redefine life:

27. Wear a piece of jewelry which belonged to your loved one, whenever you look at it, you will remember them.

Action taken on what date:
How I felt doing it:
How I feel now:
How this action has helped me redefine life:

28. On special occasions, such as birthdays or Christmas, buy a gift for your loved one and then donate it to someone who needs it, such as a homeless person. It will make their day as well as yours.

Action taken on what date:

How I felt doing it:
How I feel now:
How this action has helped me redefine life:

29. Put a bench in your garden or in the cemetery garden with a plaque on it which says in memory of your loved one and a few words about them.

Action taken on what date:
How I felt doing it:
How I feel now:
How this action has helped me redefine life:

As you struggle to redefine your life, you are in the process of creating a new path for yourself. It will be a struggle of back and forth, doing what you don't want to do, feeling like you don't have the energy to do any more, wanting to just give up and quit. On one hand, you want to complete the above-mentioned activities; on the other hand, you know it means letting go of the life you had before. As you take action, you gain hope. Hope is what opens the blinders to the thoughts that you can have a future. When you are grieving, it's important to have hope for your future. You hope that eventually your pain will cease; that you will find renewed strength; that as you struggle to redefine your life, you are in the process of creating a new path for yourself.

WALLS AND DOORS

As we begin our journey of life, we enter a life cycle that seems to be somewhat predictable. As infants, we learn that basic needs will be met for us. As children, we experience the goodness of those adults responsible for our care. As adolescents, we learn that doing good to others will result in them doing good to us. We are taught that as adults, if we study well, work hard, and love those who love us, things will turn out for the good. As we grow into senior adults, we have learned that no matter what, the sun will rise in the east, the ocean waves will pound the beach, and the grass will grow in the garden. Then, in a shocking second of time, all those natural patterns of goodness and predictability change when we are told a loved one has died. Our orderly world has changed, and we are not prepared. We are not ready to comprehend how, why, where, and who it involves. The wonderful cycle of life is disrupted, and we are left trying to sort out the consequences. Grief begins the moment you look in the mirror and don't recognize the person staring back at you. The moment you begin to grasp that life is never going to be the same. The sun will rise, the ocean will have waves, the grass will still grow, but your world has stopped. As we work our way through the grief process, we must pick up on the barriers and overcome them. We are learning the hard lessons of "good emotional" days and "bad emotional" days. There are warning signs of walls that are fundamental sticking points to prevent recovery and helpful doors to aid in recovery.

Walls and Doors
I feel empty.
Devoid of emotions.
Not knowing if I am coming or going.
At times, I have embraced it;
These walls that hold my pain.
For the comfort of my walls,
Had become so familiar,
I could not envision a release.
Like a cloud of empty promises,
It covers me in darkness.
Numbing me with sadness.
Draining color from my life.
But I am promised a door,
A person, a sign, a common kindness, an uncommon God.

WALL—PROLONGED ANGER

Anger is a common and even necessary response to loss. However, prolonged anger that turns into rage events becomes a wall against recovering. When we lose people in our life, we have good reasons for anger. Anger is a warning sign that states something is not correct, it is not normal for our life, will not be beneficial for our long-term stability. Rage is an unhealthy response to our life situation.

Rage will victimize you and those around you. It will build a wall that others will be so uncomfortable; it will increase your sense of isolation. Try a one-hundred-day plan to decrease the prolonged anger.

Each day be determined to give up one percent of your anger. When we have a plan and work the plan, then the plan works. Each day spend five to ten minutes writing in a journal. (1) Make the daily heading state "My anger is at _______% today and I will decrease it to _____% today. (2) Then document who, what, where, when, and why your anger is focused for this day. (3) Read your responses out loud and be as angry as you can possibly be in that moment. (4) Then state all the reasons for not forgiving the object of your anger. (5) Pick out one of those reasons for not forgiving and state that, just for today, to get one percent less angry, you will forgive that one reason. One hundred days later, you can be a new person. It will not take away the pain or provide a substitute for the object of your loss. It will provide you a plan to break down the wall of prolonged anger.

WALL—DANGEROUS DEPRESSION

I feel so depressed over my life situation that I can't and won't do things I normally would do. I see life as not worth living and sometimes go as far as to begin thinking how I would hurt myself. The depression is obvious to others. I quit eating correctly. I don't fulfill a daily schedule of normal activities. I am convinced God doesn't care about me or my situation.

I go through the motions of life as if I were an actor in a play. Life has no control. I may daydream and feel something will rescue me from this situation. A sense of failure begins to develop. "Magical thinking" is used. I want things to work out or get better without doing anything to make them better.

What are symptoms of depression and when does it become dangerous?

According to the National Institute of Mental Health, symptoms of depression may include the following:

- difficulty concentrating, remembering details, and making decisions
- fatigue and decreased energy
- feelings of guilt, worthlessness, and/or helplessness
- feelings of hopelessness and/or pessimism
- insomnia, early-morning wakefulness, or excessive sleeping
- irritability, restlessness
- loss of interest in activities or hobbies once pleasurable, including sex
- overeating or appetite loss
- persistent aches or pains, headaches, cramps, or digestive problems that do not ease even with treatment
- persistent sad, anxious, or "empty" feelings
- thoughts of suicide, suicide attempts

Are there warning signs of suicide with depression?

Depression carries a high risk of suicide. Anybody who expresses suicidal thoughts or intentions should be taken very, very seriously. Do not hesitate to call your local suicide hotline immediately. Call 1-800-SUICIDE (1-800-784-2433) or 1-800-273-TALK (1-800-273-8255) or the deaf hotline at 1-800-799-4TTY (1-800-799-4889).

Warning signs of suicide with depression include:

- a sudden switch from being very sad to being very calm or appearing to be happy
- always talking or thinking about death
- clinical depression (deep sadness, loss of interest, trouble sleeping and eating) that gets worse
- having a "death wish," tempting fate by taking risks that could lead to death, like driving through red lights
- losing interest in things one used to care about
- making comments about being hopeless, helpless, or worthless
- putting affairs in order, tying up loose ends, changing a will
- saying things like "It would be better if I wasn't here" or "I want out"
- talking about suicide (killing one's self)
- visiting or calling people one cares about

Remember, if you or someone you know is demonstrating any of the above warning signs of suicide with depression, either call your local suicide hotline, contact a mental health professional right away, or go to the emergency room for immediate treatment. The depression over the loss has become dangerous.

Answer the following questions aloud to a responsible adult and answer "Yes" or "No". The purpose of this exercise is to verbalize thoughts and feelings on really hard issues.

I feel sadness inappropriate for my situation?
I don't see any future?
I feel I have failed more than the average person?
I am dissatisfied or bored with everything?
I feel guilty all of the time?
I feel I am being punished?
I hate myself?
I blame myself for everything bad that happens?
I have thoughts of killing myself?
I have difficulty crying when sad?
I feel irritated that I am alive?
I have lost interest in others?
I can make no decisions?
I believe I should die?
I find myself unable to complete what's expected of me?
My sleep pattern is irregular—too much or not enough?
I am too tired to do anything?
I have an irregular appetite?
I have lost significant weight?
I am worried about my physical health?
I have lost my faith?

WALL—AVOIDANCE

I avoid my responsibilities, because I am grieving. I avoid people who will point out my behavior. When they do, I get angry and try to explain that I deserve to feel the way I do. I try to take the focus off of me and tell them they just don't understand. I begin to create problems for myself by using poor judgment and impulsive decisions. I feel uncomfortable around others, I spend more time alone. I increase my loneliness and isolation behavior. I want to just give up on living. We need others, but we are afraid of what they will say. Instruct them by having them read this section of the book as they interact with you:

There are some unhelpful things that people can say during this time of grief.

1. Don't try to tell me that you understand my pain. You do not know what it is like to be me at this moment in time. Don't say, "I know how you feel," because you don't. No matter what pain you have endured, you can't relate to my experience of pain. Comments like this make me feel that you do not understand the enormity of the blow I have experienced.
2. Don't tell me that you know things will work out for the better. How can you know the future? I can't see past this moment. The future is a scary place for me right now. My whole world has been rocked to its foundation. It will take time for me to start processing the life changes I will endure.

3. Don't try to tell me how I should feel, how I should act, or how long it will take for me to recover. I have never experienced this before. I am not prepared to feel, act, or recover at this time. It would be unhealthy to put off grieving, feeling, or start recovery before I have had a chance to experience my grief.
4. Don't give me spiritual answers or tell me I will be stronger for enduring this problem. All I know is that no medals are given for enduring pain. I don't want easy answers to complicated life-altering questions. You cannot explain why I am experiencing this trauma and why certain people are "chosen" to endure these traumas. I do not want to be one of the chosen. Choose your Bible verses very carefully and ask yourself if this will give me comfort or condemnation. I already feel condemned by God, and I don't need your help to further my thoughts about my life situation.
5. Don't tell me terrible stories of people you know who have experienced something similar to what I am going through. Are you trying to make me feel better or worse? I know that you are just keeping conversation moving forward, but this is not helpful.
6. Let me struggle with the following questions: What people, places, and activities am I avoiding? What seems to be my fear of these things?

WALL—CONFUSION

I have trouble clearly thinking through problems and developing solutions. Sometimes my mind races, and sometimes it moves too slow. I can't seem to remember simple details. I go from no reactions to overreacting. I feel as if I am going crazy. I am making bad decisions. I am angry with people, because they don't seem to understand how I am. I feel as if I am losing control. I can't seem to cope anymore. I become scared and panic at the thought of what's happening to me. I have difficulty deciding what to do next in order to manage my life. Sometimes our thoughts can get us stuck and confused. It is helpful to challenge our irrational thoughts. Our confused thoughts often fall into one of four categories:

1. My life isn't fair and hasn't turned out the way I wanted
2. My life is over and my path will not turn out right.
3. I will never be the same, so I can't go on.
4. I feel so guilty that I am the one left to live.

Thoughts like these if left to spin in our brain can be unhealthy and self-destructive. These confused thought patterns will lead to anxiety and depression. Being stuck and confused is part of the grieving process. Living stuck and confused is part of a choice for irrational thinking. Ask yourself these questions: (1) What would my loved one want me to do? (2) What small but reasonable change can I make today that will help me get unstuck? (3) What helpful suggestions are my significant others saying to me that I know are true?

> The truth that many people never understand, until it is too late, is that the more you try to avoid suffering the more you suffer because smaller and more insignificant things begin to torture you in proportion to your fear of being hurt.
>
> —Thomas Merton

WALL–GUILT

I have a deep sense of shame, because I believe I did something that caused their death. I can't trust God with this issue. In fact, I play God, as if I could have prevented this tragic situation. Because of my shame, I can't take care of myself. I don't believe I did the best I could do in that situation. I may have made a mistake and can't accept I wasn't perfectly in control of their situation at all times.

"Healing the Guilt and Shame"

> "I was the driver in a tragic car accident in which a 17-year-old girl later died on Christmas Day. Although I wasn't speeding (35 mph) and drugs and alcohol were not a factor, I was distracted for an instant and ran head on into an oak tree which stood only two feet from the road. We had seven people in the car and none of us were wearing seatbelts. There were multiple injuries throughout the vehicle.

While still in ICU, the horrific and shocking news of the girl's death devastated me. A few days later, I would discover that her father was killed three years earlier in a car accident. Once out of the hospital, I visited the girl's mother and through our tears, she immediately forgave me. In fact, after all this woman was going through, she was comforting me. Nine months later, her 15-year-old daughter was also killed in an unrelated car accident. To this day, the mother and surviving family members define endurance as well as any human being(s) can. I have found strength through their resolve.

One of my biggest mistakes following our accident was my refusal to talk about it. It felt like a sense of nobility in carrying the pain with me. At this time, I actually wanted the burden because I felt I deserved it. Over the next several months, I spiraled downward emotionally into deep despair, a bottomless dark pit of depression caused by relentless guilt and shame. I fell in love with my sorrow, too. Pity can be such a dangerous partner. In another crucial mistake in trying to grieve or cope with Tina's death, I chose alcohol to numb and dull the pain. I had grown up in an alcoholic atmosphere, but in no way was that an excuse. I drank just like anyone does. I chose to. Though alcohol can initially dull our emotional pain, it also dulls our passion for God. But as long as I avoided the pain, I avoided healing. And God wouldn't heal what I continued to avoid. I struggled with humanity's biggest addiction of all-the addiction to self.

In the years to come, I would discover that recovery is an ongoing passage to freedom.

Over the next several months, I would be hospitalized three times for the formal treatment of depression which included two sets of ECT treatments. After a suicide attempt, I was then voluntarily placed in Florida's state hospital in Chattahoochee, Fl for a period of five months. It was there, in the heart of the utmost in mental anguish, where I first experienced God's peace. Through praying/reading/counseling/listening to Christian music/solitude and time, I slowly began to understand the divine aspects of God's love, grace and forgiveness.

Too many people suffer needlessly from unresolved guilt and shame. Often, it is our misunderstanding of their divine dynamics that prevents us from living in a liberated and Godly lifestyle. Guilt and shame are normal, healthy and necessary emotions, intended to guide our behavior like a check and balance mechanism. Appropriate guilt and shame leads to redemptive desire and helps prevent the perils of self-absorption. Both guilt and shame are divinely designed to be instructive in nature. Unfortunately, many people tend to take guilt and shame to their extremes, being burdened by the weight of them, or possibly worse, having no guilt and shame at all. We live in a culture that far too often lacks shame.

Guilt can be very difficult to resolve because of so many potential inner payoffs that most of us are unaware of i.e. an unconscious pleasure from suffering, and a sense of connectedness to someone who may have died. Similarly, guilt (survival) can be an after-the-fact expression of loyalty to the dead. In survivor guilt, we can feel our healing is at the expense of the person who died, while also feeling the wrong person died or survived. Our grief process can be further complicated because we may prefer to feel guilty rather than to feel lonely, empty or helpless. Many people shy away from releasing themselves from guilt and shame because by doing so, they feel it doesn't honor the depth of their wrong doing. Before we realize it, guilt can evolve into just another form of self-indulgence.

A healthy sense of shame can actually be a form of humility before God. It can also be an invitation to grace. Toxic shame, on the other hand, is based on things outside of ourselves, i.e. the flawed perceptions of others or self, primarily due to rejection, betrayal and broken trust. It is a relationship wound that often feels like a wound made from the inside. It was once described as a hemorrhage of the soul. Toxic shame breeds in silence. We may crave external affirmations for our internal shame. Generally, guilt is what we feel when we make a mistake. Toxic shame can make us feel we are a mistake.

The only thing that can conquer our false sense of guilt and toxic shame are God's grace and forgiveness. Indeed, forgiveness is the most powerful experience a human being can have, but it is also often the most misunderstood. In fact, we only discover our sense of identity and value through God's pardon alone. He never asks us to extend more grace and forgiveness, even to ourselves, than He has already given us. When we refuse to forgive ourselves (or others), we are giving ourselves higher standards of forgiveness than God. We are also choosing to remain a victim. And as long as someone else is responsible for our behavior, we will never get better. Refusing to forgive is the destruction of joy. Forgiving ourselves is taking a bold step into power.

Tragedy never has to have the last word. Christ's resurrection from the darkness of death is our basis of hope in the midst of tragedy. (Acts 2:23-36). Hope, once defined as a memory of the future, eventually comes to terms with tragedy and heartache. So often, trust may start on the dark lonely side of painful and what may feel like unbearable circumstances. If we allow Him, God will recycle our grief and any emotional baggage and transform it into an instrument for redemption. (Eph. 1:7).

Jesus chose to drink the cup of redemptive and creative suffering. He chose a path leading into the teeth of suffering (John 10:17-18). As the brilliant French philosopher, Simone Weil, once said: "The extreme greatness of Christianity lies in the fact that it does not seek a supernatural remedy for suffering, but a supernatural use for it."

Our suffering ceases to be suffering once we can give meaning to it. Our joy is born in sorrow. Indeed, in God's time, our deepest hurts can become our greatest gifts. God freely gives us the power of choice. Between guilt and grace, Christ chose grace. Let us choose wisely..."

From: Tragic Redemption: Healing the Guilt and Shame. (Langmarc Publishing 1-800-864-1648) By Rev. Hiram Johnson, LCSW.

DOOR–HONESTY

You are not God. You are not in control of all situations twenty-four hours a day. You are to accept your situation and are to work through it. You are to roll with the rides of grief. You are to share your grief with those who try to understand. It is perfectly acceptable for you to share with others what you need at this time in your life. It doesn't mean others will agree, understand, or even comply with your requests. All you can do is to be honest with the present moments. Sometimes it is helpful to your own honesty if you prepare a letter to be given to those significant others in your life. It can look something like this:

> Dear_______
>
> As you know, I have suffered a terrible loss in my life. I am grieving and do not know how long the process will take for me to begin to reengage in any sort of life style. I know that I am in the process of trying to understand my loss and what life will be on a day to day basis. I want you to know how much I appreciate your support and understanding during this time in my life. I would ask you to be aware that I am

not always in control of my emotions. If I am rude, uncaring for you, or make bad decisions concerning you during this period I ask that you would give me grace and mercy.

More than anything else, I ask that your presence be a gift to me, as I am comforted that someone cares about me. I know that you do not know what to say to me and it presents an awkward situation for both of us. Please continue to reach out to me.

My loss is the only thing I can think about. I am sorry that I am not available to give to you right now. I know that I will begin a process of recovering as I face my grief, but I need for you to know that I have not established a time table for recovery.

Thank you for being my________. Please know that your thoughts, prayers, caring, and helpful things you do for me do not go unnoticed. I may not notice right now but I am sure that God notices.

Love,___________

DOOR—GET WITH PEOPLE

Join a group of sorrowing people who can relate to your experience. Seek professional counseling. You need new friends who have been through your experience.

Our fear about getting with others is that our grief will overwhelm them, they won't know what to say to us, and they are concerned about driving us deeper into our grief. We can open the door to their help by simply instructing them on some things they can say that will be helpful to us.

> The capacity to give one's attention to a sufferer is a very rare and difficult thing; it is almost a miracle.
>
> —Simone Weil

They can do two things right: they can come and be with us, and they can listen with understanding.

Teach them to use phrases as they listen:

Tell me more
Help me understand
I can see your pain
I don't know any answers but I am here with you
I wish I could take your hurt away
I am praying for God to ease your painful journey
I agree that it is not fair for you to have this much pain

DOOR–CARE FOR YOURSELF

Bereavement can be a threat to your health. At the moment, you may feel that you don't care. That will change over time. You are important to God. Your life is valuable. Do purposeful work and activity. Eat well. Exercise regularly. Find a purpose in life if only temporary. Postpone major transitional decisions. Record your thoughts in a journal. Most people who are grieving find it helpful to journal. Writing helps to express the feeling and emotions that are inside. What should you write about? Anything you want to write about. Here are some suggestions: your thoughts about your loss, their abandonment of you, your relationship with God, your relationship changes with others, different memories, the things you didn't get a chance to say or do.

"Excuse me, I'm grieving."

> "Recently, two of my closest friends died. The first friend fell off a windmill; the other killed himself. Both of these deaths left me feeling devastated, yet, a common response I received from friends was: "It happens in threes."
>
> I am not usually a sympathy-seeker, but I would have benefited from a friend's visit, flowers, a sympathy card, a meal, any of those traditional gestures that are made when a family member dies. Anything but a warning that there is one more death to come.
>
> When I called a close friend to tell her about the man who had killed himself, her first response was: "Good, now he can't bother you anymore." This man and I had been friends for six years and his infatuation was only a recent development. I was already plagued by guilt; this did nothing to ease my conscience. Then she went on to say: "Do me a favor. Don't call me for at least one day. I'm tired of your grieving."
>
> The friend across the street said: "The writing was on the wall." The last time I saw this man, he was working on his will, told me he was considering suicide, and we talked about his depression. He made an appointment with a

doctor, but the appointment was a six day wait. The writing was on the wall, and I left him alone. This seems unforgivable, and once again I felt reminded of my oversight.

I had been friends with the man who fell off the windmill for about twenty years and was financially unable to fly in for the funeral. One friend wrote me a letter to say everyone was there but for three of us, whom he listed by name.

When we arranged a memorial for the suicide friend, many people didn't know who I was and asked if I was the woman he had just broken up with? The impetus for him killing himself? One man even asked if I couldn't have gone to bed with him a few times just to keep him alive. No one understood the guilt I am now plagued with; they were just trying to understand why a seemingly healthy man would take his life. Even I didn't know the depths of the depression he had been experiencing for over half of his life until I found his journals. By then, he was dead.

The next thing that happened with these deaths was that people started to think I may be depressed, even suicidal. My father's wife wrote me a letter encouraging me to not do anything "irrational." Thus far, that has been my best bit of advice.

I called the suicide help line just to talk about my grief. The volunteer interrupted my crying to ask if I was eating. Eating? Wanted to know how many hours a night I was sleeping. Sleeping? Wanted to know if I was alone.

Suggested I go to a hospital for the night. I tried to assure her that I was with my young daughter and had no intentions of killing myself. I called hoping she could absolve me of the guilt I was feeling, the same way I imagine Catholics do with their priests.

I have learned to tell people "I'm grieving." This puts a distance between us, but lets them know I intend to grieve, recognize these losses in my life, and not be expected to carry on as they may hope. My writing class students had to call to remind me they were waiting for class. I apologized for not remembering the day, but didn't say, "I was grieving." They are senior citizens and probably understand what I am going through since they are facing many losses in their lives.

For two weeks, I was busy meeting my suicide friend's family, clearing out his apartment, writing his obituary. Those tasks are finally done. This week I try to have nothing planned every other day so I can be home where I can grieve in peace. Every other day, I need to get out, be with friends, take a swim, see a movie, share a dinner.

Grieving eases my guilt and pain. Grieving allows me time to feel sad, a healthy reminder that I am compassionate. Grieving forces me to accept my losses. Grieving scares away the people who seem to think grieving is peculiar. My grieving may never end, but it will diminish in time. One day my vulnerability will disappear and I will be able to say, "It really doesn't happen in threes." One day."

Author Unknown

There are a number of things we can do when we are opening the door to take care of ourselves.

- Try to identify and process what it is that doesn't make sense about your loss.

  Is it unfair? Is the timing wrong from your perspective? Does it bring up your own questions about God? About life? About your death? Write in a journal the answers to these questions.
- What emotions overwhelm you on a daily basis? What triggers these emotions? What have you done in the past that's been helpful to you to deal with loss? Who has been helpful to you? Who allows you to express these emotions without feeling overwhelmed themselves? Who doesn't? Are you getting too much into the following: I should have! I could have, if only? Leave these for later on in your recovery, as this is not helpful to you now.
- Use the "one helpful thing" rule for each day. What one action will you take today to help yourself move forward? Identify it and complete the task.

  You need to see yourself in a moving forward position. One forward movement a day will process a feeling of success, and you will be able to build on the chance. Everyday needs to be one change forward toward restoring your health.
- Become reflective on your own life

This loss affords you the opportunity to take a pause in life. Use the opportunity well. Your loss has gotten your attention in this fast and fleeting life. This can be a time of reevaluation in your career, your location, what you see as a ministry, what you hope to accomplish in life. Use this loss to make a commitment to make your life count. Write out your dreams and goals. What one thing would you like to have accomplished one year from now?

DOOR—STOP ASKING WHY?

Give up the three questions that begin with "why." "Why did I...?" "Why did they...?" "Why did God...?" You have already asked these questions a million times. This is the way life is for now. We cannot change what has happened. It has happened. It is historic fact. Everyone who grieves is bound to ask these questions. There are no concrete answers. We can speculate. We can make stuff up that sounds good. We can try to create reasons to offer comfort to ourselves and to others; but in the end, we just don't know.

In this aspect, basic religious truth must come into the picture. To ask "why" on a repeated basis is to blame God for letting it happen. If we take a good look at biblical truth, we can learn that God does not let us explain why He did things. We dare not make excuses in approaching God. The author of the book of Job deals with the question of "why?" Job cried out and asked God why all these things happened to him, a godly and upright man. The book deals with the suffering of one who is innocent and does not deserve all these losses. Finally, when Job understood, he would be challenging God to continue the protest; he was able to change his whole approach and ask that God teach him. This is when Job began to heal and to be restored. It is the same process for all persons.

"Why?" has to be abandoned in overcoming grief as well as in understanding the nature of one's own conduct. "Why?" never appears in the creed of any religious faith and is certainly not in any form of confessional. Nor is it found in the Lord's Prayer or the Ten Commandments.

So "why, why, why?" has to go, and the focus must be placed on one's own changing.

This is illustrated in a story about two battleships assigned to the same area in the ocean for training maneuvers. They had been in rough seas for several days, with terrible visibility, huge waves, steady pelting rain, dark clouds, and an all-consuming fog. After another long tension-filled day, it turned into a pitch-black night. The lookout on the portside of one battleship reported a light bearing toward them on a dangerous collision course. The captain called out to the signalman, "Signal the approaching ship to immediately change course before we collide." The signal came back, "I advise you then to immediately turn away." The captain, fearful, commanded, "I am a captain, you immediately change course." The signal back, "I am a seaman second class, "You better immediately change course." The captain, who by this point was beyond fear and was filled with rage, commanded. "I am a battleship. I command you to change course." The reply, "I am a lighthouse, I know what's best for you, change course before you crash on the shore." We can spend too much time asking "why?" and only end up crashing on the shore.

DOOR–CLEAN HOUSE

Time alone will not heal grief. You have to deal with it to work through it. In the process you can actually transmute grief into personal growth. You can become something *more* than you were. Consider the following ideas.

- Build on your memories. Though you must accept your loved one's death, you need not sever all ties. You can use memories to establish a new kind of relationship, and you can find ways for those memories to enrich your life.

"I Didn't Want To Say Goodbye"

"My dearest husband,

I love you, and God how I miss you. I saw a television show the other night and they talked about how you should write a letter to someone who has died to help deal with unresolved emotions. I know all that stuff but when it became a reality for me, I just didn't know what to do. I have these thoughts that go on in my head day and night and I should put them down somewhere. I feel that if I write them, I will lose you. I know that is not true but my heart hurts so.

I'll probably ramble all over the place because I think of everything, from the time we met until we had to say goodbye. Mary Ellen introduced us, and I will always be grateful she did. Right from day one you were so strong in mind and body and yet so gentle. I had so many problems in my life and later I found out you did too, but you always managed to put me first.

Remember our first apartment. You made the arrangements without talking to me. You just said we were going to live together. I was such a mess that I just followed. I know you remember that I was a lousy cook in the beginning, but you ate everything. Thank God I eventually learned how. You told me you loved me after only a couple of weeks. I told you that you would wait a long time for me to say that. That didn't bother you. I was afraid to love, everything I knew about love did not feel safe, you made me feel safe.

My sons, Chris and Dave, were 7 and 4 years old. They became your sons in all the ways that mattered. Because of all the problems I had that revolved around my drinking, sometimes you were their whole world. I don't know if I ever thanked you for just being there for my, no our, children when I could not. I am sorry to say that you and I both know that this was a lot more than I care to remember. I know we had bad times, but even the worst fade when I think about you. I love you. I like saying it and I miss saying it to you.

People tell me that I am strong—maybe I am. If that is true, it's because I had the freedom in our marriage to grow. I thought that when we were going through the first stages of my recovery from alcohol that would be the most difficult time in our lives. It wasn't, only because we were together.

The day we found out you were ill, it was our wedding anniversary. Oh yeah, remember our wedding. The kids stood up for us and then Chris got mad because he could not go with us afterwards. We should have taken them along—you got sick, said it was dinner. I knew it was fear. We argued about that for years.

There have been a lot of people in our lives, not one of them has ever made me feel as safe and confident as you always did. I'm scared right now but when I think about you, I work through it.

We got to see two of our kids married. Jere, well, he will get there. My God, he is so much like you. I found a lot of comfort in that in the first few days after you were gone. The day we found out about the cancer, I can say the word now, we were oblivious to the fact that our world was about to cave in. We even prepared ourselves for a situation of your having had a mild stroke and as you put it, we would cope.

I was so frightened, God knows you must have been terrified. Yet, you would not let me see you cry. In fact, you asked me outside the medical building why I was falling apart. You said I had to straighten up because if you could handle it, so could I.

Did you know after that, when I wanted to cry, I would go upstairs and put my face in a pillow so you could not hear me. You probably let yours out when I was out of the house—I hope so anyway. I have done a lot of mini crying as I call it. Nothing gut level, but I know it is there trying to get out. I hate this grieving stuff, it seems so selfish. I think of all the reasons I want you alive and most of them are about me. I like the way you took care of me and let me think I was taking care of myself. I knew you were a good husband, I told you I loved you—just wish I had said it more often.

I long for the times we used to pat each other on the rear end when we would pass each other going from one room to the other. Remember how we would lock the door on a Friday night and not go out again until Monday morning. I miss our little world we lived in. I am also angry for you, John. The fact that you never got to do what you wanted to do. You know—buy that boat. I kept telling you to, but you wouldn't because I did not know how to swim. I told you I would wave to you from the dock. I'm glad we got to take the vacation we took. When we went on our first trip—it was so far away, St. Kitts. When I saw it on the map, I said I could not go that far. That changed quickly because I knew then what I know now—that I would go to the end of the earth with you and back again. Never a doubt. I'm also angry because you never asked for much, and I hope and pray that as your family we gave you some of what you needed.

When you were sick, I did not know if I could take care of you. Love really gives you a strange kind of power. I could feel your cancer—as I gave you back rubs I could feel it move on to another spot. We quietly and lovingly lied to each other when that happened.

You know I cannot forget your warped sense of humor. Those corny jokes you told. You did not lose your sense of humor while you were ill. I distinctly remember being in Wegmans and while we were in the paper goods aisle, you said, "I have been meaning to tell you that for the past 25 years you have been putting the toilet paper on the wrong way." Everyone in that aisle started laughing and they did not realize you were serious. You told me you felt better after you had said that. Well, having my spouse tell me his biggest complaint after 25 years was putting the toilet paper on the the wrong way was the greatest news I ever heard. If you could dwindle all our problems down to that, what greater love had I. Then there was the time I gave you a whistle to use to call me when you needed me. I was upstairs, you blew on that thing so hard I almost broke my neck getting down to the first floor. When I got there, our son Dave was falling over with laughter as you said, "I just wanted to show him how it worked." You took care of Chris too—thinking of something for him to do for you. You made up that story about needing him to take the air conditioner out of the window. You did not want him to feel left out because he was not living as close to us as Dave. You were concerned how he would feel later if he had not done something for you.

Jere, well the two of you shared several private moments that I wished had been longer.

We had several home aides and you didn't pull any punches there either. I guess that's what made it all seem like a dream. You kept on fighting so I never thought it would end. The supervising nurse said they talked about us at the office because we were so close. You always said it was nothing special our relationship—we always did for each other. They meant the fact you put me first even to the end. I guess if you are going to have something rub off, love is the best thing.

I always liked looking into your eyes and telling you how I loved the fact that they were such a wonderful blue. The cancer took the blue out of your eyes but I still remember.

I wish I had more time to take care of you—I thought I did. Even when the doctor told me to call hospice and I took you home from the hospital, I thought we had more time. I guess I watched too many old movies.

I wanted to be able to say goodbye in a different way. That's a lie. I never wanted to say goodbye. I did not want to have memories of Hospice telling me, your husband is significantly declining. I wanted them to do something. Instead, sometime before 4 a.m. on April 4, 1995, I was holding you and listening to sounds that I had never heard before and never want to hear again. I have since learned that they call that the death rattle. It was not my idea of saying goodbye. I told you I loved you, the kids and I would be all right. I said that because I felt you needed to hear it to let go. I wanted to scream, John, please don't leave me—don't go. But, I thank God every day for those few moments. When the sound stopped, I still held your hand.

It is six years now. Our children and grandchildren, you would be proud of. Me, well I am sure you've been watching and probably shaking your head. I will get better, just give me a little more time.

I have loved you and still love you so much that my heart hurts. I was blessed and know that I am still blessed with our family. Somehow that does not replace your being beside me, telling me to put my cold feet on yours. You always said, "I love you"—even when we had a fight. I still tell you I love you before I go to sleep because I believe you can hear me. It's the cold feet that I can't do anything about. I always pictured us as this old, old couple and people wondering what we were doing together—just as they had for the past 25 years. And, we would do as we always had, smile like we had the world's best kept secret. We did have a secret, John—it was not being afraid to love each other as hard as we did and, as we do.

I can't let go completely yet—I wrote you this letter when two years had passed. Then, I had to read it again, shed a few more tears and decide to share it with others. I thank God everyday for bringing you into my life and I work very hard at not being angry with him for taking you out of it. Please, please, please know that no one except God could love you more.

Goodbye for now my husband—keep an eye out for me.

Your wife yesterday, today and always."
Michele Humeston

- Many survivors become more involved in their loved one's work or interest. A spouse can sometimes take part in a husband's or wife's business.
- If you have literary ability, you might write in a way that is influenced by or dedicated to the memory of the one you loved. If you have the money, consider setting up a memorial fund or foundation.
- Recall the humorous times and laugh about them. Some will disapprove if you laugh "too soon," but it's not disrespectful. Remembering laughter is helpful.
- Assist other bereaved people. Find an organization through which you can be a friend to the sorrowing.
- Building on memories *directly* is not the only way to go. Realize that you may be at a kind of crossroads where new opportunities for service or involvement should be explored. This may be the time to become active in church, return to school, work with needy children, or volunteer at a hospital.

Whatever you do, do not waste your life in unproductive sorrow. The best memorial to a loved one is a full, *growing* life.

Another way to clean house is to turn the horrible situation into a positive experience.

"TRANSFORMATION"

"His clothes still hung, on their hangers, in our closet, neatly and untouched. Everything was in its usual place. How could I even think of getting rid of them? It would only leave another big void in my life. My husband had died a year ago and it was unthinkable to part with anything that was once the very essence of him.

He was a hard working, loving man, providing for his family, and his clothes, being modest and humble, portrayed this aspect of his life. I could picture him in every shirt that he wore on different occasions… his favorites and not so favorite ones. Each piece had a story to tell. Deep down, I fantasized that maybe this was all a dream and I would soon wake up to find him lying next to me again. So I shouldn't clear away his things, because he may need them! But this just hasn't happened, and who was I kidding, but myself.

I reasoned that it seemed so insensitive, to throw his clothes into a Salvation Army bin, where they would get mixed up with everyone else's castaways, or to donate them to a thrift shop for people to scrutinize and pick over…

then, to perhaps witness someone in our town wearing my husband's shirt! Maybe I could just leave them in our closet forever? That would be easy, but my life has changed dramatically since his death, and I am still here, realizing that I must move on and keep living. Nothing stays the same, even though I wish it would.

Dad's flannel shirts and winter sweaters were dispersed among our four children and myself, but our son and son-in-laws were all too big and tall to fit into his pants and cotton shirts. What could I do with them? I agonized over making the right decision. What action could I take that my conscience would allow me to live with, while gaining space in our once shared closet, soon to become solely mine? Would giving them away or tossing them out make me selfish or irreverent to his memory?

About 3AM, early one morning, an answer popped into my head. Due to my belief about death, I had come up with the perfect solution. I would make a quilt from the material in the clothing; in fact, five quilts, one for each of our children and one for myself! My belief is that, when you die, you don't ! You just change form (from body to spirit) and so it would be with his clothes. They would simply change form and be with us in a different way. This was the answer! I felt good about this idea and couldn't wait to begin the transformation!

That same day, I started: carefully cutting up his shirts and pants into the same size squares. No fancy patterns, because he was not fancy or frivolous. Each sleeve and pant leg was tenderly opened to enable me to cut the flat pieces that I needed, without a seam. I was especially careful to keep his shirt pocket in tact in one of the squares, where I would eventually tuck a laminated, heart shaped photo of each child with their dad, which also had a message on the back that stated, I'll always be with you. This would be attached to the pocket square with a gold cord, pinned to the inside, so it couldn't drop out, and from each article of clothing, I collected every button for my button box, which I inherited from my grandmother (a beautiful frugal women) and my children would someday inherit from me.

The colors and patterns were artfully coordinated into harmonizing groups and were sewn together with much thoughtful concern. Then, they were backed with a super soft fleece material and lightly stuffed with batting. Lastly, they were quilted with floss of a complimentary color and each priceless photo was placed in its respective pocket square. They were striking, simple and honest—an array of irreplaceable memories, with the added sense of touch!

When the quilts were finished, the children came to the house to get them. We sat around, each one eager to try out his special blanket, as we deeply pondered every square, recalling its happier past. Within a few minutes, we began to notice something unusual—an extreme warmth that oozed from them. They seemed to exude a heat that was intensely soothing to the soul, yet so much hotter than we would have imagined any quilt could possibly produce. We immediately knew that it was Dad's energy and the warmth of his love, that we felt, then, and every time since, that we've used them.

I don't mind the emptiness in the closet, as I thought I might, knowing that when I need to be hugged and comforted, I can snuggle under my precious quilt to feel cozy, safe and loved, because his clothes haven't really vanished, they are still here with me… like him, they've just changed form."

Author: Avis Kaeselau

DOOR–RETURN TO GOD

Perhaps through the grief process you feel very far from God? Perhaps you doubt God? Perhaps you are angry with God? That's all alright, as long as you are willing to return to God. Now is the time to test and exercise the concept of spirituality.

Spirituality is not religion. Religion is man trying to get to God. Spirituality is God coming down to man and developing a relationship. This relationship was developed through the person of God's only son—Jesus Christ. Once we have this relationship established (repentance), it's a forever deal. Because it doesn't depend on who we are, but on who God is.

1. Spend time reading in the great grief book of the Bible—the book of Psalms.

   David, the author, was a man well acquainted with loss and grief. He wrote some of the most beautiful pictures of human suffering that we have in any literature. People frequently see themselves as they read in the Psalms.

2. Try to pray.

   It will not come easy as you share your sorrow with God. God understands when our prayer is nothing but a screaming, weeping, questioning prayer. He promises that He can handle it. He knows what we are doing, and it doesn't take Him by surprise. If you are frustrated, angry, anxious, depressed, sad beyond belief, and wondering where to voice it, the right place, the right time, the right God is available to hear your pain.

3. Remember when God was close to you in the past.

   You may have to think past your present hurts to a different time and place in your personal history. What did it feel like then and not now? How did God come to you to help? Remember that He doesn't change. If He helped you, then He will help you now, and He will help you in the future.

The book *Recovering from The Losses Of Life* by Norman Wright, has valuable insight into our recovery process and the role that God plays in our long-term recovery. He states, "You may not feel that God is doing anything to help you recover. Why? Because we want recovery now. The instant-solution philosophy of our society often invades a proper perspective of God. We complain about waiting a few weeks or days; but to God, a day is as a thousand years and a thousand years as instant. God works in hidden ways, even when you and I are totally frustrated by His apparent lack of response. We are merely unaware that He is active. God has a reason for everything He does and a timetable for when he does it. Give yourself permission not to know what, not to know how, and not to know when. Even though you feel adrift on the turbulent ocean, God is holding you and knows the direction of your drift. Giving yourself permission to wait can give you hope. It is alright for God to ask us to wait for weeks, months, and even years. During that time, when we do not receive an answer and/or solution we think we need, He gives us his presence" (Wright, 1991, pp.136–137).

4. Explore the past, present, and future. Use these helpful open ended statements to get started on your journey of recovery.

ABOUT ME

My biggest struggle right now is:
The thing that really gets me down is:
This is what I feel I have lost:
When I feel lonely:
The thing I most fear:
The most important thing I have learned:
The thing that keeps me from moving on:
I seem to cry most when:
The reoccurring dream is about:
This is how I have become stronger:
A new person I have come to appreciate is:
I get angry when:

Part of the past that keeps haunting me is:
What I have learned from the past is:
I need you to somehow understand:
The experience I miss most because
of what has happened is:
The changes I most dislike are:
Guilt feelings happen most when:
I need you to know:
I don't ever want this to happen:
My feelings sometimes confuse me when:
My biggest disappointment in myself came when:
My worse day has been:
My best day was:
I smelled something that made me think:
I saw something that made me think:
New experiences that I enjoy the most are:
I am angry when:
I am discouraged when:
For me, to find balance, I:
I got a call, e-mail, or letter from _____and it meant a lot
to me:
I know when I am most lonely because:
I felt panic when:
I know I will find hope when:
If I could say a prayer today it would be:

BIBLIOGRAPHY

Blackaby, Henry, *Experiencing God* (Lifeway Publishing, Inc.1998), 73-74.

Bridges, Jerry, *Trusting God* (Navpress, Inc., 1992), 154-157.

Bowlby, John, *Loss* (Basic Books, Inc., 1980), 93.

Carlson, D, *When Life Isn't Fair* (Harvest House Publishers, 1989), 38.

Collins, G, *Christian Counseling* (Thomas Nelson, 2007), 112-115.

Claypool, J, *Tracks of a Fellow Struggler* (Insight Press, 1995), 53.

Dodson, James, *When God Doesn't Make Sense* (Tyndale House Publishers, Inc., 1993), 40-59.

James, J., *The Grief Recovery Handbook* (Harper and Row Publishers, 1988), 132-133.

Kushner, H., *When Bad Things Happen to Good People* (Avon Books, 1981), 128.

Kellerman, Joseph, *Grief* (Hazelton Educational Materials, 1977), 3-4.

Lewis, Gerald, *Critical Incident Stress* (Accelerated Development, Inc., 1994), 1-8.

Lucado, Max., *In The Eye of The Storm* (Thomas Nelson Publishers, 1991), 108-111.

Lucado, Max, *No Wonder They Call Him The Savior* (Multnomah Press, 1986), 105-106.

Morris, S., *Overcoming Grief* (Basic Books, 2008), 185.

Peck, Scott, *The Road Less Traveled* (Simon and Schuster, 1978), 15-16.

Rando, T., *Grieving: How To Go On Living When Someone You Love Dies* (Lexington Books, 1988), 281-281, adapted

Seamands, David, *Healing for Damaged Emotions* (Victor Books, Inc., 1981), 58-59, 75-76.

Yancey, Jerry, *JOB* (Navpress, Inc., 1992), 205-210.

Wood, Barry, *Questions Non-Christians Ask* (Fleming H. Revell Company, 1977), 25-31.

Wright, Norman, *Recovering From The Losses of Life* (Guideposts, 1991), 136-137.

Wright, Norman, *Crisis and Trauma Counseling* (Regal Books, 2003), 232-234.

Wright, Norman, *Experiencing Grief* (Broadman and Holman Publishers, 2004), 18.